13·12·17

Sir, Although I do not know
I was forced to engage in this secret-
                    Santa game,
Taking name from hat, I thought for a while,
About gifts I could buy without cramping
                    your style,

Sir, This pointless, silly game, you see,
Is nothing but a mystery,
My identity shall remain ...
So.

Sir, I wish you a Merry Christmas,
New Year, and Good Health
From THE one and only.
Stockbridge Village Christmas Elf!

CW01560618

This book is dedicated to Charles Wotten, and to all those black men and women whose sacrifices have played such an important part in the development of Liverpool's social and cultural identity.

Great War
to
Race Riots

Writing on the Wall
Toxteth Library
Windsor Street, Liverpool
L8 1XF

Published by Writing on the Wall 2017
© Madeline Heneghan and Emy Onoura

Design and layout by Katrina Paterson
ISBN: 978-1-910580-19-6

All rights reserved. No part of this publication may be reproduced,
stored in a retrieval system, or transmitted, in any form or by any
means, electronic, mechanical, photocopying, recording or otherwise,
without the prior permission of the publishers.

0151 703 0020
info@writingonthewall.org.uk
www.writingonthewall.org.uk

Contents

Acknowledgements

The Great War to Race Riots archive is based on a collection of letters and documents which were originally part of the Lord Mayor's correspondence. It was rediscovered by Joe Farrag, a local history enthusiast, who, having recognised the significance of his find, shared it with Writing on the Wall (WoW) after observing the ground-breaking work of our George Garrett Archive Project. We gratefully acknowledge his important role in bringing this significant and historically important collection into the public domain.

With the support of the Heritage Lottery Fund, Writing on the Wall launched a new project which focused on the collection and its social, economic and political contexts. A team of volunteers, who formed the Great War to Race Riots Archive Group, researched, catalogued and digitised the archive. The team are: Vicki Caren, Janet Johnstone, Sharon Lane, Catherine Leen, Margaret Millne, Suzanne Morris, Marmura Nyirenda, Janaya Pickett and Rose Thomas. Special thanks to them for their enthusiasm and commitment to the project in preparing the collection for digitisation on a dedicated website and for public access at the Liverpool Records Office. Our thanks also goes to Liverpool City Council's Archivist Helena Smart for her specialist guidance and support.

Against the background of continuing cuts by central government to local authority funding, this collaboration between communities and public services, a model devised by the George Garrett Archive project, has important historical material which might otherwise have been lost or forgotten. Due to the support of all those involved, this archive is now available for public view in Liverpool's Central Library.

For her research into the lives of the men named in the Great War to Race Riots Archive, we are indebted to Kathy Donaldson, an expert in World War I family history. Thanks is due also to Michael Mahoney of the National Archives at Kew for his assistance in locating a range of documents held within their archive, but also for his genuine passion for delving into the subject.

We met Stephen Rigden at the *Who Do You Think You Are?* Family History Show, held at the Birmingham National Exhibition Centre. Stephen volunteered to assist us in our research and was able to trace living relatives of three men in the archive: the Bynoe, Bjorkhaug, Cargill, Nimbley and Santos families. We are grateful to Stephen for this work, and to the families for their ongoing support for the project and the production of this publication.

Creative responses have also helped build a more complete vision of the lives and the sacrifices made by black servicemen in World War I, and shed light upon those in Liverpool identified through the work of the project. Thanks for this aspect of our work goes to internationally acclaimed poet Levi Tafari, whose poem, 'A Letter of Concern', is included in this publication, and was produced as part of a specially commissioned body of work in response to the archive. Levi also supported others to respond creatively to the letters through a series of public workshops. Thanks also to award-winning visual artist Faith Bebbington, who led in the community creation of a Black Poppy sculpture, a special commission by Culture Liverpool as part of the 'Weeping Windows' exhibition of poppies at St George's Hall, which were originally displayed at the Tower of London.

Special thanks is also due to Mike Morris, Co-Director at Writing on the Wall, for his invaluable advice and guidance, both in delivery of the Great War to Race Riots Project and in the writing of this publication; labour historian Tony Wailey, and Dr Andrew Davies of the Department of Geography & Planning at the University of Liverpool, for their encouragement and suggestions, and to WoW Trustee Maura Kennedy for her scrupulous proofreading. Finally, thanks to the WoW team, particularly Katrina Paterson, for her beautiful design work, but to all in the WoW office who have suffered the inevitable trials, tribulations, moans and groans, throughout the writing process.

Madeline Heneghan, Writing on the Wall Co-Director
Emy Onuora, Author

A Letter of Concern

The Town Hall
Liverpool
13 May 1919

Dear Home Secretary in Parliament London
I am writing this letter to you
I have had a visit from the Ethiopian Association
I need your advice on what to do

Six hundred African British subjects
are stranded here in the city of Liverpool
they are anxious to return home to Africa
as their treatment in the city by the locals is tantamount
to cruel

Though many of them have served in our armed forces
they have strange practices not to mention their culture
many have married British women and have children
some say the races should not mix they find this practice
vulgar

Speaking for myself I would just like to say
this is not the way I think
but if this situation is not resolved soon
our city will soon be on the brink

Companies won't employ coloured men
as employers and the trade unions conspire
to uphold segregation in the work place
integration is not what they desire

I am caught in the middle which way should I turn
I say pay them five pounds and then repatriate them
it's a small sum to pay for their return
to relieve us of this Black irritation problem

Can you give my concern your urgent attention
I beg your haste in dealing with this matter
these coloured men bring out the worst in our men
these black men are destroying our culture.

I am Sir
Your Obedient Servant

John Richie

Lord Mayor

P.S. Our city would once again be light, bright and all
right!
    And did I mention all white.

Levi Tafari
May 2014

Introduction

The Great War to Race Riots archive is a rediscovered collection of letters and documents which forms part of the Lord Mayor of Liverpool's correspondence from 1919, following the demobilisation of the armed forces after World War I. The documents, dating from 12th May 1919 to 9th November 1920, relate to the position of black ex-servicemen, seafarers and factory workers in Liverpool, who were destitute, some even stranded, due to conditions which will be described in this book. The archive presents the unheard voices of the period and uncovers the heritage of Liverpool's black community. Ongoing research has located a host of families living in Liverpool and the UK who are directly descended from some of those named in the archive.

The collection includes a list of eighty-two names and addresses of black workers and servicemen compiled by the African Christian Association.[1] It includes letters and testimony from men from Africa, the Caribbean and India, who had fought for England on land and at sea during the Great War, or had worked in factories to support the war effort. In eloquent hand-written appeals to the Lord Mayors of Liverpool, black colonial subjects, some with local wives, partners and children, describe the competition for jobs in post-war Liverpool, which rendered them unemployed and unemployable when a colour bar is imposed following the demobilisation of white soldiers. They express incredulity that foreign white workers are being employed in preference to black British citizens who have served in the war or supported the war effort. They describe themselves as 'patriots' who are still willing to serve 'God, King and Country'; their sense of injustice and desperation is palpable.

The correspondence between the men themselves, their advocates at the African Christian Association, and the Lord Mayor of Liverpool, describes their experience of casual racist abuse and warns of increasing racial tensions, which subsequently exploded into full blown race riots on the streets of Liverpool in 1919.

It was not only in Liverpool that popular racism translated into race riots during that year. Other seaports saw violent anti-black rioting. Glasgow's was the first in January, followed by South Shields in February, with London witnessing serious levels of violence from April to August. In June, Newport and Barry saw rioting, while in the same month Liverpool and Cardiff experienced the worst rioting of the year. In Cardiff, three men were killed, two white and one black, with many more badly injured. In Liverpool, serious levels of violence against black people were recorded from May 1919, with a full-blown riot beginning on 3rd June resulting in the murder of Bermudian seafarer, Charles Wotten.[2]

This post-war phenomenon of race riots was not restricted to the UK. In the United States, in what became known as 'Red Summer', such riots occurred in more than three dozen cities and one rural county. In both Britain and the US black communities fought back fiercely with a determination to assert their rights as citizens who had contributed as much to the war effort as white servicemen and workers. These race riots, and the black reaction to them on both sides of the Atlantic, were symptomatic of post-war working class dissatisfaction, which was expressed not only in racial terms but in class terms too.

The causes and nature of the riots in Liverpool and

their aftermath have been explored fully by historians and sociologists. Working class radicalism, competition for jobs, and threats to white masculinity, have all been cited as key factors, though to different degrees depending on interpretation. Evidence has been drawn from police and court reports, newspaper articles and communications between government offices, along with the memoirs of Ernest Marke[3] who was a victim of the rioters, or 'John Bulls'[4] as he termed them. Whilst the value of Marke's testimony should not be underestimated, the fact that it was written over fifty years after the events should be taken into account.

The Great War to Race Riots archive brings the voices of black workers from 1919 and 1920 into the centre of the discourse. It gives personal insights into poverty and discrimination through the words of the men themselves who, in their entreaties for intervention by the Lord Mayor, reveal their experience of living through incredibly violent and turbulent times. These are not begging letters; rather they articulate a sharp sense of injustice at their treatment as British citizens who had come to defend the motherland, or who were considered good enough to fill the war time labour shortage, only to find themselves impoverished and abused in post-war Britain. The archive also reveals the sympathies of some white Liverpudlians and the concerns of the British establishment for their colonial empire and trading interests. This fear was not unfounded, as news of events in Liverpool and other port cities in the UK travelled and fed into demands for home rule in the colonies.

The response of the British establishment to the plight of black communities in British seaports, evident in the Great War to Race Riots archive, was to pass responsibility between local and central government, the Home Office, the Colonial Office and the Ministry of Labour, revealing both a level of incompetence and deeply entrenched institutionalised racism. The newspapers of the time employed the same inflammatory ideas and language as the modern tabloid press when railing against immigration. In local and national media, the black community across Britain is portrayed as a criminal class, both aggressive and 'childlike' and, most vociferously, as sexual predators. The abhorrence displayed towards the interracial marriages and relationships that naturally occurred in the port cities clearly demonstrates that racist ideologies - developed as justification for the brutality of the transatlantic slave trade and refined during the colonial era - defined the experience of black people in post World War I Liverpool.

The Great War to Race Riots archive adds to our understanding of Liverpool today: the conditions and issues the black community faced following World War I have shaped the experiences and characteristics of the present black community. It contains important lessons for modern Britain, where xenophobia is rising and the demand of 'British jobs for British workers' is not just one of the far right but is promoted by a government in crisis. Clear parallels can be drawn between today and 1919 in that order is partially maintained through the creation of a racialised scapegoat. The focus on immigration and the use of the popular press as a vehicle to blame the ills of society on the 'outsider' is a classic combination which seeks to shift the focus away from a ruling elite, whose concern is not the welfare of the masses but the protection of capitalism and the drive for profit.

The Formation of Liverpool's Black Community

The development of Liverpool from a minor fishing port surrounded by farmland and small villages to the British Empire's foremost mercantile and trading centre was rapid. During the 18th century, Liverpool's population grew from 5,000 to 78,000 and the city, in turn, grew wealthy and prosperous. This expansion was made possible by the city's involvement in the transatlantic slave trade. The city's growth fuelled Manchester's cotton trade, Lancashire and Yorkshire's mill industries, Lancashire, Yorkshire and the Midlands coal industry and ultimately, Britain's industrial revolution.

Liverpool belatedly entered the slave trade in 1700 when the *Liverpool Merchant*, under Captain William Webster, delivered 220 enslaved Africans to Barbados, where they sold for £4,239.[5] Trade to Africa was administered and monopolised by the Royal African Company until 1698, when it released its iron grip on this lucrative trade by opening it up to all. The company charged 10% on all goods imported, except for redwood which carried a 5% duty; gold, silver and slaves were free of all duty.[6] For the next hundred years or so, massive profits from the transportation and sale of millions of Africans enabled the port and the city of Liverpool to grow in wealth, population, trade and prosperity.

Britain had vied with its European rivals, most

5

notably the Portuguese, for dominance of the slave trade until it finally and decisively took the upper hand in 1713 under the Treaty of Utrecht. Under this agreement, Spain ceded Gibraltar and Minorca to Britain; more significantly, it gave Britain the right to supply slaves to Spain's American colonies, including South and Central America, the Spanish West Indies (for example, Cuba, Santo Domingo) Florida and Mexico, at the rate of 4,800 slaves per year.[7] Britain emerged as the world's foremost slave trading nation, responsible for over half the trade by the beginning of the 19th century.

Investment in these ships was undertaken by an array of small businessmen, craftsmen and clergymen, but alongside these small investors were the rich and powerful with their close ties to local government and parliament. By the mid-18th century, Liverpool had overtaken Bristol as the major British slave port, with dozens of registered ships ranging from vessels that could hold 50 slaves to larger ships that carried over five hundred. Almost every mayor and MP during this period had significant commercial interests in, or family ties to the slave trade. The Liverpool brand 'DD' that was burned onto the bodies of slaves was a guarantee of 'prime quality', mainly used on children from 6-14 years of age.

The city's wealth grew on the trade in African slaves and slave-produced cotton, sugar and tobacco. By 1789-91, over half of all slaving ventures were accounted for by the seven largest firms, led by William Neilson, John Shaw, William Forbes, Edward Philip Grayson, Francis Ingram, Thomas Rodie and Thomas Leyland, all with significant links to local government and parliament. Later, the larger slave merchants diversified into banking and insurance.

Liverpool merchants undercut their rivals in Bristol

and London by slashing expenses and overheads. They employed boys rather than adults and paid crews once per year, thereby reducing prices by about 12%, or £4-5 per head.[8] Slave ships were generally recognised as the most brutal vessels in an industry already noted for its brutality. They were essentially floating factories, with an extremely high death rate among its cargo of slaves, and an even higher one among the not so valuable crew.[9] Amongst Africans, three boys in twenty and one girl in five did not survive the journey from Africa to the Americas, and by 1784-90 the death rate among crews on slaving voyages was one in five, twice that of its human cargo.[10] Due to its brutal nature and year or more long voyages, recruiting to slave ships, despite the fact that sailors were amongst the poorest occupational groups of the 18th century, was difficult. Slave ship captains were largely sadistic, maintaining discipline by beatings, floggings and mutilations.[11] Tropical diseases, exacerbated by poor diet and callous disregard, accounted for the huge death rate. However, hunger and poverty were the biggest recruiters to slave voyages and the death rate meant that, for those who stayed alive, promotion could be virtually guaranteed.

The vast majority of Africans were sold for plantation slavery, although some found their way to Liverpool as trophies and rewards for ships' captains and officers. These enslaved Africans were used mainly as domestic servants and advertised for sale in Liverpool newspapers and coffee houses. Servants were one of the largest occupational groups in 18th century England and, as the century wore on it became ever more fashionable to employ or own black servants. In addition to domestic servants, Liverpool's burgeoning black community was supplemented by free blacks, such as seafarers, sons and daughters of rich African traders sent to England to study, and refugees from the American War of Independence. The latter group were former slaves who had fought on the British side and had migrated to Liverpool to avoid charges of treason that would almost certainly have resulted in their deaths.[12]

In 18th century Liverpool, therefore, not all blacks were enslaved. In addition to many of the freed blacks arriving in Britain after the War of Independence, many of those held in slavery in Britain were able to gain their freedom and many more escaped into poor and black communities in London and other cities. Estimates of the size of the black population during the 18th century varied wildly. Some estimates were politically motivated and used as ammunition for both sides in the increasingly bitter war between the pro- and anti-slavery lobby, while newspapers deliberately exaggerated the numbers of blacks in Britain in order to frighten its readers. Most historians agree that it was around 15,000 by the latter half of the 1700s.[13]

As the century progressed there were more free black people in Britain than slaves. Many had asserted their freedom by escaping into a life of hardship and poverty, but also liberty, in preference to the more certain but enslaved life of domestic servitude. This poverty became a feature of British life and the 'black poor' became a much commented upon social problem. Many blacks were beggars and vagrants who no doubt were involved in petty crime as a result. The severe winter of 1786 led to the establishment of a 'Committee for the Relief of the Black Poor', whose role was to raise monies to address the problem. The committee metamorphosed into raising money to repatriate black people to areas of West Africa still dominated by the slave trade.[14]

As the horrors of the slave trade became more widely known, due in part to the personal testimonies of freed slaves such as Olaudah Equiano,[15] the opposition movement grew. Those who campaigned for abolition on humanitarian grounds formed the bulk of the abolitionist movement, which included many Quakers, Methodists, and other clergy. Campaigners such as William Wilberforce, and Liverpool's own William Roscoe and William Rathbone, were drawn from this tradition. A second group of abolitionists, including chartists and other radicals, were driven by political radicalism and an ideology which argued that liberty for blacks and whites was indivisible. Liverpool's Edward Rushton formed part of this tradition. He had served on slave ships and on one journey contracted ophthalmia which would later render him blind. Repulsed by the treatment he witnessed of Africans destined for slavery, he became one of the fiercest opponents of the trade.

Working class solidarity with enslaved people was also a feature of the abolitionist movement, demonstrated by the Lancashire mill workers who boycotted slave-produced cotton despite it resulting in their own severe hardships.[16] Petitioning was also a popular form of working class radicalism and in the 1790s over one hundred petitions opposing slavery were submitted to Parliament. The sustained pressure from this movement had a lasting impact on the political elite, making it impossible for the issue to be easily dismissed. Terrified by both the French Revolution and the slave revolt in Haiti, the establishment feared the connection between domestic radicalism and abolitionism. Many also expressed concerns that petitions were signed by the uneducated and lower orders.[17]

Resistance to abolition was at its fiercest in Liverpool, not surprising given the degree to which those who benefited most from the trade were also prominent in local and national government.[18] In 1787, thirty-seven of forty-one councillors had extensive connections to the slave trade. Ten years later, thirty-four of thirty-eight councillors were slave ship owners, suppliers or investors. Throughout the period of organised opposition to the slave trade (1787 - 1807), all twenty Mayors of Liverpool had been at some time either owners of slaving vessels or holders of shares in slaving ventures. The importance of the slave trade to Liverpool's development is reflected in the architecture of its Town Hall; built in 1754, its façade is adorned with caricatures of Africans alongside elephants.

The city's political and merchant class were inextricably linked, and formed the most extensive opposition to the anti-slavery lobby. John Tarleton, a leading Liverpool slave trader, spent over three hours in 1788 attempting to persuade Prime Minister William Pitt of the need to maintain the trade.[19] Liverpool could be a dangerous place for abolitionists who were constantly threatened with acts of violence. Even as organised opposition to slavery grew, Liverpool's political and merchant class contained both pro- and anti-slavery elements, with many abolitionists still involved in the trade. William Rathbone, for example, was a founder member of the Liverpool Committee for the Abolition of the Slave Trade while his trading empire was built on American slave-produced goods.

For many decades, the prevailing view was that abolition was achieved through the campaigning of humanitarians such as William Wilberforce. However, most progressive historians now accept that the changing economic system, which relied on wage labour and free market enterprise, was a crucial if not *the* crucial factor in the abolition of slavery.[20] While the abolition movement challenged slavery on an ethical level, it was ultimately its decreasing profitability, due in the main to the changing economic system and accentuated by the cost of slave rebellion and sabotage, that rendered the system obsolete.

The slave trade was officially abolished in Britain's colonies in 1807 and effectively ended in 1865 by the American Civil War. However, the triangular trade's most pernicious legacy, the ideology of racism, survived. This is not to suggest that race prejudice did not exist prior to the trade in Africans, but that the concept of race, and ideas about the inferiority of black people, were crystallised during slavery into a systematic set of beliefs in justification of the trade; the first form of slavery in which slave and master were defined by their skin colour. Peter Fryer makes an important distinction between race prejudice and racism:

> Race prejudice is relatively scrappy and contradictory. It is transmitted largely by word of mouth. Racism is relatively systematic and internally consistent. In time, it acquires a pseudo-scientific veneer that glosses over its irrationalities and enables it to claim intellectual respectability. And it is transmitted largely through the printed word[....]The primary functions of race prejudice are cultural and psychological. The primary functions of racism are economic and political.[21]

An early and very influential text in the development of race as a concept and racism as an ideology is Edward Long's *History of Jamaica*. Long, a member of the British plantocracy, injected pseudo-science into his theory that Africans are less than human. Such thinking was validated within scientific and other academic institutions in 18th century Britain. Both the Church of England and the Roman Catholic Church were quick to uphold this

11

rationale for slavery. Clergymen were quick to reassure slave owners that conversion to Christianity would not interfere with property law, property in this case being the enslaved African.[22]

Slavery had generated huge profits that rapidly boosted the rate of industrialisation. Increasing this necessitated high efficiency through free trade and free labour. This began to render slavery uneconomic. In addition, Britain moved into a period of colonial dominance as Africa and other territories were partitioned and fought over by European powers. Consequently, Liverpool reinvented itself from a fierce and often violent supporter of slavery into a city that promoted its diverse and cosmopolitan character, and was proud to host a colonial exhibition in 1886 celebrating its role as gateway to the empire. However, it was fundamentally a celebration of British dominance in transnational commerce and white supremacy over colonial subjects.

Liverpool, Gateway to Empire

The century prior to the outbreak of World War I has been described by historians as 'Britain's Imperial Century'. In this period, Britain moved toward the direct rule of whole nations as colonies, as well as exerting its military, political and, most fundamentally, its economic influence over its dominions and protectorates. From 1776, following the American War of Independence and the loss of thirteen North American colonies, India became far more significant to the empire. After the Indian rebellion of 1857, termed the 'Indian Mutiny' by the British, India was directly ruled by Britain, becoming its 'Jewel in the crown'. Later in the period came the scramble for Africa, which by 1914 saw 90% of Africa under European rule, with only Liberia and Ethiopia remaining as independent territories. At the onset of World War I the British Empire was the largest in history, comprising 14 million square miles of territory and a population of 450 million people. Colonists proudly claimed that due to its vast expanse, the sun never set on the British Empire; contemporary Chartist and socialist Ernest Jones countered that, 'the sun never sets, but the blood never dries'.[23] Despite renewed attempts to give the empire back its respectability, violence, forced labour, torture and mass murder were its hallmarks.[24]

In contemporary Britain, the empire is often viewed with nostalgia and regret, a condition described by Paul Gilroy as 'postcolonial melancholia'.[25] In recent years,

13

politicians from across the spectrum, most notably Gordon Brown and David Cameron, have given new credence to the Churchillian position that empire brought civilization to ignorant and inferior peoples across the globe. It's unsurprising then that contemporary opinion polls indicate that almost half of the UK population regard Britain's past colonial empire as a good thing.[26]

Colonialism, defined simply as the conquest of territories and control of its goods, is not a uniquely British, nor indeed European phenomena. In *Colonialism/ Post Colonialism*, Ania Loomba cites the examples of the Aztec Empire in Central Mexico, the Mongol conquest of China and the Moorish invasion of Spain, along with numerous other instances of early colonialism and empire building. However, because it was established alongside capitalism, she regards the modern colonialism of Western Europe as having the capability to exert a much more profound effect on the countries it conquered:

> Modern colonialism did more than extract tribute, goods and wealth from the countries that it conquered – it reconstructed the economies of the latter, drawing them into a complex relationship with its own so that there was a flow of human and natural resources between colonised and colonial countries. This flow worked in both directions[....].[27]

The port of Liverpool was pivotal in that flow, for the purpose of empire was not to bring enlightenment to the dark reaches of the globe but rather the acquisition of raw materials such as sugar, cotton and mahogany, and the destruction of colonial industries to enable the forced purchase of manufactured goods from the colonial power. Liverpool, having established itself as the European capital of the transatlantic slave trade, was able to position itself as a key port through which the materials and commodities of empire flowed. Historian turned politician, Tristram Hunt, in his *Ten Cities of Empire*, a well-researched account of colonial cities, which nevertheless descends into a veiled justification of empire, vividly describes the internationalism of Liverpool's commercial interests:

> The *Red Book of West Africa* was Liverpool's in-house directory of those many merchants running operations in and out of the four British colonies of Nigeria, Gold Coast, Sierra Leone and the Gambia and by the early 1900s the African Section of the Liverpool Chamber of Commerce was one of the city's most powerful lobby groups. Soap production was just one of a number of new businesses growing up around the Liverpool Import trade: close by there were the cigarette makers rolling tobacco leaf from South Africa, mills grinding Canadian grain and Indian rice and sugar refineries like Tate & Lyle refining West Indian cane for the biscuit business.[28]

Liverpool merchant families were also key players in the Caribbean. The Booker family and their role in British Guyana exemplified the scope of Liverpool's trading interests and influence in the British West Indian Colonies. The Bookers, after which an avenue in Liverpool and the Booker Prize for literature are named, had owned sugar plantations in Guyana since the early 19th century. Having been compensated £2000[29] (worth over £188,000 today) for the loss of their slaves following abolition, and with their already well-established fortune, the Bookers were well set up to take advantage of the new era of free market enterprise. By the end of the 19th century, the

Bookers owned most of the sugar plantations in Guyana and played a leading role in the economic history of the colony, especially from the beginning of the 20th century. By the middle of the century, the company owned large holdings in Trinidad, Barbados and Jamaica, as well as in Canada, India, Belgium, and East and West Africa. The Bookers' impact on the economy of the country was so great that Guyana, then known as British Guiana, was often referred to as 'Bookers Guiana'. [sic][30] The Royal Bank of Liverpool and the Royal Insurance Company were founded on the back of profit made on Guianese soil.

As well as providing plentiful and cheap materials, the colonies also provided sources of cheap labour for use in the colonial territories, and in Britain too. Though the colonial territories covered continents encompassing vastly different peoples, cultures and systems, the political, social and economic subjugation of the colonial territory and the exploitation of its labour were common features. The 'Gateway to Empire' therefore offered an apparent escape from the harsh conditions of imperial rule, causing Liverpool's black community to increase and diversify.

During the 18th century, estimates of the size of the black population in Britain ranged between 3,000 and 20,000.[31] It had grown throughout the 18th century, particularly during the mid-century era when slave trading was at its peak. Whereas in the late 17th and early 18th century, members of Britain's black community were characterised as domestic servants to fashionable and prosperous households, their growing numbers rendered them less exotic, and they began to be employed in occupations lower down the social scale. The majority of Liverpool's black population in the early 20th century were colonial subjects or their descendants.

Certainly, the men named and those whose words are contained in the Great War to Race Riots archive came from the Caribbean, Africa and India.

From the 1870s onwards, Liverpool shipping firms began to dominate the UK trade from West Africa, employing crew from Sierra Leone, present-day Nigeria, Ghana and the Gambia. In 1876, in what Jaqueline Nassy Brown describes as 'a watershed moment',[32] the Elder Dempster Shipping Company was formed in Liverpool through the amalgamation of firms already trading with West Africa and 'some of shipping's most powerful moguls',[33] thereby allowing Liverpool to monopolize the trade in West Africa. The Elder Dempster line hired thousands of West African seafarers who were paid at lower rates than white British seafarers. Black seafarers, though in lesser numbers, were also employed in the British West Indies by the West India & Pacific SS Company, which later became the T&J Harrison line. Others, such as City Boats, employed lascars, a loosely defined description originally applied to seafarers of the Indian sub-continent, later expanded to include those from Burma, the Yemen and the Middle East, so that the shipping company could pay them at the lesser lascar rate. While non-white labour was cheaper, there was also the pseudo-scientific belief that Africans, like the South Asian lascars, were more suited to heat, and therefore the sweltering conditions below decks.

By the late 18th century, Liverpool's black community, which was overwhelmingly male and poor, resided mainly in the area around the docks commonly known as 'Sailortown' and less commonly as 'Darktown'.[34] It was also home to other immigrant communities, including Chinese, lascars, Irish, Scandinavians, Italians, Americans and many others. Their numbers were constantly swelled by seafarers from all over the world looking for

17

lodgings, food, drink and entertainment. Fire regulations prevented ships' crews from staying aboard while in port, and so 'Sailortown' was peppered with taverns, brothels and gambling dens to serve this clientele. The area was remarkably cosmopolitan, with high degrees of social integration between different racial and ethnic groups. Black US seafarers in particular enjoyed a kind of freedom unseen in the USA, including having relations with white women that would most likely have them fearing for their lives at home.[35]

Seafaring dominated the fortunes of Liverpool's black population and was to do so for the next 150 years. It provided the main sources of income for the city's black community, and determined its location amongst the city's poorest housing in close proximity to the docks, from which the majority of black men drew their employment.

The development of steam required sailors to possess different skills from sail-powered ships. Men worked in extremely high temperatures and harsh conditions in engine rooms: trimmers provided a constant supply of coal to the furnaces that created the steam to power the ships; 'firemen' or 'stokers' stoked the furnaces while 'greasers' oiled the machinery below decks. Shipping companies like Elder Dempster began to use wholly West African crews whilst ensuring that captains and officers were white. Black seamen were overwhelmingly employed below deck in jobs that were amongst the lowest paid. Seafaring was casual work and when black seamen where laid off they found it harder than their white counterparts to get another ship. Harder still was finding work ashore, as white seamen often rejected black men as shipmates and white dockers refused to work alongside them.

Nevertheless, black workers began to settle in

Liverpool due to several factors. Higher wages were paid to seafarers who set sail from Liverpool and other British ports rather than from West Africa. In addition, there were some opportunities for employment outside shipping, and many settled into relationships with local Liverpool women. These interracial marriages and relationships attracted the attention of those responsible for upholding standards of morality and decency. Talk of liaisons and marriages between blacks and whites were quickly reduced to discussions about sexual activity in a way that relationships across class or national lines never were. Issues of love, respect, endearment and affection were never discussed. They were viewed as primarily sexual relationships. Although there was evidence of interracial marriages and relationships occurring among the aristocracy, commentators only denounced 'the lower orders of women' for their relationships with black men.[36]

Frequently in receipt of lower wages and far more susceptible to the economic highs and lows of industry than white workers, black communities were generally characterised by low income and poverty. The scale of poverty in Liverpool was so acute that a committee was established in 1880 to provide relief to black seamen found destitute in the city. A 1910 Parliamentary Committee survey into 'Distressed Colonial and Indian Subjects' acknowledged the grave economic circumstances of black communities, and found that discrimination against seamen in employment, lower pay and exclusion from trades and workplaces, were well-established practices.

The National Sailors' and Firemen's Union (NSFU) was originally opposed to the inclusion of 'foreign' workers, but eventually changed its position in response to the shipping companies' use of black seamen to undercut the wages and conditions of its members. In 1911, the NSFU held a mass strike as part of a wider general transport strike involving dockers and railway workers as well as seafarers. The NSFU's demand for official recognition was won, as well as a higher union rate of pay for both British and 'foreign' seafarers. However, as most black seafarers remained outside of the union, shipping firms like Elder Dempster were able to partially offset the wage rise for white seamen through a reduction in the wages paid to African crew members. Ships' articles after 1911 show that white wages increased from £3.10s to £5 per month, while those of African firemen reduced from £3.10s to £2.10s per month.[37] In 1916, the Ministry of Shipping announced national wage rates, but 'Asiatics and coloured ratings', which had previously been below the standard rate, were excluded.[38] This pay disparity was formalised with the establishment of the National Maritime Board in 1920.

Although seafaring trades dominated the employment experiences of black communities, it was by no means the only area of employment available to blacks. Unlike in the City of London after 1731, where it was decreed that black people were not allowed to learn a trade, no such explicitly organised bar to employment existed in Liverpool. Many worked as butlers, nannies and other roles in domestic service. Others were employed in trades and some owned lodging houses. There were students and professionals, many of whom formed a key role in the development of the first black political organisation in Britain, The Pan African Association, which was founded in 1900. Amongst its activists was John Archer from Liverpool, the son of a Barbadian father, who was a ship's steward, and an Irish mother. Archer was elected Mayor of Battersea in 1913, only the second ever black mayor, and was a member of the African Progress Union (APU), which in 1918 campaigned for black political representation.

The cosmopolitan dockland areas, where the black community mainly resided, was home to people whose heritage could be traced from around the world. To support increasing settlement, a number of sailors' hostels and boarding houses were established in the dock area around Pitt Street and Stanhope Street, some directly owned by Elder Dempster specifically for its crew. By 1911, although the area around Parliament Street and south docklands formed the main hub of the black community, over half lived in other parts of the city, even as far as Scotland Road to the north of the city centre. The *Liverpool Catholic Herald* described the dockland area around Mill Street and Beaufort Street as a 'no-go' area characterised by, 'lodging houses for negro, lascar and other foreign seamen, mulatto children, drunken men and women and street fights. These streets are not considered desirable beats by the police.'[39]

The period at the turn of the century was one of great concern about the threat of competition for work and the undercutting of wages from Eastern European immigrants, overwhelmingly Jews fleeing pogroms and religious persecution. Fuelled by anti-immigrant sentiment and anti-Semitism led by politicians and the press, the 1905 Alien Act was introduced, which restricted the numbers of foreigners from outside the empire that could come into Britain. The act didn't affect black workers significantly as it didn't seek to redefine British nationality. The impact of this for Liverpool and other port cities and towns fell mainly on Chinese seafarers. However, there was an increasingly inflammatory and racist discourse, exemplified by the *Liverpool Chronicle*'s description of migrant labour as, 'scum left by the tide of migration between Europe and the continent of America'.[40]

By the late 19th century, Liverpool's black population, through immigration and the birth of a new generation was second only to that of London as the largest black community in Britain, a position it was to maintain until the Second World War. But its reputation as competition for white employment often gave rise to conflicts, as well as unofficial barriers to certain employers and trades.

Defending the Motherland

The colonies played a crucial role during World War I as the British clamour for patriotic support resounded throughout the empire. Ironically, notions of duty to the motherland existed alongside notions of racial inferiority and the subjugation of colonised people, but while war reinforced racism and the imperial hierarchy, it also challenged the colonial set up and brought about resistance to the prevailing world order.

The colonies provided a critical source of labour and materials. The African continent, which by 1914 was almost entirely under European rule, became a major theatre of war. The first shot fired by a British serviceman is now believed to have been in Togoland, by Alhaji Grunshi of the Gold Coast Regiment.[41] At the outbreak of war, Britain called upon her colonies to help her support the war effort, as did other European powers on both sides of the conflict. Many men, and a fair number of women, answered the call, leaving their homelands to contribute as soldiers, sailors, labourers, nurses and other roles. Nearly 1.5 million Indian soldiers and over 16,000 men from the West Indies fought and served.

As well as supplying men and women, colonial citizens raised thousands of pounds to send directly to Britain to support the war effort. Barbados, for example, in addition to military support, offered the British government £20,000 in money or sugar. As a result, around 1,000 tonnes of sugar was shipped to England

and contributions from the island were repeated annually for the duration of the war. It is estimated that approximately £80,000 in cash and £20,000 in sugar was contributed to the war effort and nearly £30,000 raised by Barbadian charities. Trinidadian oil production tripled to meet war time demand. In all, the West Indian colonies contributed nearly £2 million from tax revenues and voluntary donations. India contributed around £200 million to the war effort despite enduring higher taxes and rising prices, causing hardship which was to be exacerbated by the monsoons between 1918-19.[42]

From a modern-day view of colonialism, perhaps the most obvious question to ask is why subjugated peoples would fight, work and raise wealth for the oppressor nation in a war that was not of their making. The answer is complex. Firstly, it was partly through participation in the war that colonial peoples became fully aware of the racism and oppression which upheld the colonial system. As David Olusoga observes:

> It was during wartime that black people from parts of Africa and the West Indies gained new and first-hand experience of the racism and racial hierarchies that both informed and, for many, justified colonial rule. In ways that were not easily foreseeable when the armies marched to battle in the summer of 1914, the First World War led to the temporary lowering of the physical, cultural and legal barriers that had been erected between the races and between the subject peoples of the empire.[43]

Furthermore, in the run-up to war, powerful establishment propaganda in the media and at mass public meetings portrayed Britain as the defender of liberty and equality. Ironically, in the West Indian colonies, the emancipator of slaves, resulting in what Olusoga describes as a temporary 'war fever' on the same scale as displayed in any English town.

The effectiveness of such propaganda is clear in the letters of the men within the Great War to Race Riots archive, who frequently express their patriotism and allegiance to the crown.[44] Such patriotism was encouraged by liberal nationalists who believed that support for the British war effort would be rewarded with moves toward self-governance and home rule. Jamaican nationalist Marcus Garvey, on behalf of The Universal Negro Improvement Association, sent a telegram to the Colonial Office in London 'express[ing] our loyalty and devotion to His Majesty the King, and empire...pray[ing] for the success of British arms on the battlefields of Europe and Africa, and at sea.'[45] Gandhi, the most celebrated of Indian nationalists, called upon Indians at home and those resident in Britain to 'unconditionally' support the motherland and the empire.[46]

Many of those who signed up to war were not motivated by patriotism or nationalism, but by basic human need. Economic conditions in the colonies were the push factor for thousands of recruits across the empire. The majority of recruits from the West Indian colonies were plantation workers and artisans. Of the first 4,000 men enlisted into the British West Indies Regiment (BWIR), 1,033 were labourers, 657 were cultivators, 356 carpenters, 245 bakers, forty-two police constables and forty teachers.[47] War seemed to provide the escape from the poverty of irregular employment, low pay, injustice and casual violence, which characterised the lives of the colonial worker.

Whatever the motivation, the desire to sign up for active duty was evident. However, sections of the British establishment, most notably the War Office, were far from grateful, and often wholly opposed to black people joining the armed forces. The reasons behind the opposition to black enlistment were multiple, but in the main the idea of black soldiers taking up arms against whites, even a white enemy, was abhorrent to the colonial mentality. As Ray Costello summarises:

> At the beginning of the First World War there was a good deal of trepidation about the use of colonial troops to fight against white troops, especially on European soil, due in part to the prevalent belief in a racial hierarchy, with white Europeans at the top and black Africans at the bottom and any encouragement of 'lesser breeds' to fight Europeans was difficult to countenance. It was felt that colonial troops gaining experience in a modern war, killing Europeans, could lead to rebellion against their colonial masters[...].[48]

In addition, there were two further conflicting concerns expressed about black combatants. On the one hand, they were portrayed as incapable of effective military combat, while on the other, there was a worry that black soldiers would actually outshine their white counterparts. Adding further confusion to the colonial standpoint on black combatants was the pseudo-scientific theory of the 'martial races', which defined some nations and tribes as particularly suited to fighting and war and others as not. Such thinking determined which nations or territories should provide fighting men, and which the labourers of war who were restricted to menial work. From South Asia, the Nepalese and Punjabis were deemed to be inherent warriors and in Africa it was the Sudanese. Conversely, across the battlefields of Europe, Chinese men were employed to dig thousands of miles of trenches, a highly dangerous non-combatant role.

Some sections of the British Establishment, including Winston Churchill, argued in favour of the use of black soldiers in Europe, citing the success of France's black colonial battalions on the Western Front. Harry Hamilton Johnson, noted colonial administrator and explorer, was an ardent campaigner for the use of black troops. His position illustrated a common paternalistic form of racist thinking on the matter:

The physical strength and wellbeing of the Whites is superior in the average to that of the Blacks and Browns; and of course, their education is far more universal and advanced. When all these circumstances are taken into consideration it will be found that the Negro, Negroid and Polynesian have played a part in the war quite proportionate to their opportunities and means; and actually, would have done much more to help the allies against central powers had they not been restrained for one reason and another by their white guardians, advisers and administrators.[49]

At the outbreak of war in 1914, colonial subjects took matters into their own hands and travelled to the UK where they were drafted into a number of units in the British army. Most men financed their own travel to Britain but some were assisted by the Citizens Contingent Committee, which was set up in Trinidad and Barbados in 1915 to provide funds for any men wishing to join up overseas but were unable to do so due to financial constraints.[50]

Despite the men's determination to display their loyalty and bravery, the War Office tried to stop black men from the Caribbean enlisting, threatening to repatriate any who came. The Colonial Office had other ideas, fearing that the exclusion of colonial subjects would undermine its authority in colonial territories. It took the personal intervention of King George V for the War Office to relent, and in 1915 the British West Indies Regiment (BWIR) was formed by Royal Warrant. With a few exceptions, it was agreed that West Indians would be recruited on the same terms as British soldiers. Initially, the War Office limited the BWIR's participation to labour duties, but as casualties among the troops rose sharply, soldiers from the BWIR saw active duty.[51] A total of 15,600 men served in the BWIR during the war. Two-thirds came from Jamaica, with the rest from Barbados, Trinidad and Tobago, the Bahamas, British Honduras, Grenada, British Guiana, the Leeward Islands, St Lucia and St Vincent. In August 1915, over 2,000 Barbadian men joined the BWIR, more than the initial agreed quota required from the island. From these, just over 800 were selected and sailed to Europe, the Middle East and Africa.

In Liverpool, locally-born black men and those who were resident, enlisted and served in all branches of the armed forces. Within the Great War to Race Riots archive, the list of the eighty-two men presented by the African Christian Association to the Lord Mayor in 1920, details men who were unemployed and destitute, with some resident in the workhouse. These men served in the Cheshire Regiment, Third King's Liverpool, 26 Middlesex, Gold Coast Regiment, King's Own Royal Lancashire, and the Royal Engineers. Although a 'Coloured Section' of the Royal Engineers existed, only two men are identified as being in that battalion. The list also details men who had served in the Royal Navy and the Merchant Marine in wartime.[52] Ernest Quarless, born in Liverpool to John Quarless, a merchant seaman from Barbados who served throughout the war, and Elizabeth, the daughter of a Jamaican sailor, managed to enlist in the British West Indies Regiment in July 1917 aged 11 years and 9 months, although it is unclear if he saw action.

While black British-born and long-term resident soldiers had been a feature of the British Army long before the outbreak of the 1914 war, the debates surrounding the use of colonial troops in Europe began to impact on recruitment policy in Britain, with some recruiting officers accepting black volunteers and others refusing to do so.[53] In 1915, Tom Oroma, a Nigerian included on the list compiled by the African Christian Association, was medically examined at Birkenhead, and, although there are no ailments recorded in the examination, it was determined that he would 'not be likely to become an efficient soldier'. Despite this assessment, Tom Oroma served in the Warri Rifles, the Cheshire Regiment and the merchant navy during World War I.[54]

Black troops, like their white counterparts, fought bravely and well in Africa, the Middle East, Europe and other arenas in terrifying and inhuman conditions. Servicemen from the BWIR won military honours, including five Distinguished Service Orders, nine Military Crosses and a host of other medals and honours, as well as numerous mentions in dispatches. Despite military regulations outlawing black men serving as officers, footballer Walter Tull became an officer who led white troops, earning their immense respect and that of his commanding officer.[55] Walter Tull was mentioned in several dispatches and was killed on the battlefield in Favreuil in France in 1918.

The Indian Army played a huge role in World War I. At the beginning of the war the British Army in India sent professional Indian soldiers to Europe and Mesopotamia. Approximately 1.3 million Indian soldiers served in World War 1. Of these, 74,000 died and as many were

were wounded. In the first battle at Ypres in the autumn of 1914, Indian junior soldiers were largely responsible for halting the German advance. Letters written home from the trenches tell of the painful experiences of these soldiers, the harsh climate, the feeling of dislocation and the tragedy of war: 'The shells are pouring down like rain in the monsoon', wrote one, 'The corpses cover the country like shaves of harvested corn', wrote another.[56]

In the merchant navy, black seamen, who were mainly employed below decks as firemen and therefore particularly vulnerable to torpedo fire, suffered huge casualties. The Elder Dempster line, which routinely employed many West Africans, particularly below decks, suffered high casualty rates of both ships and crew. Elder Dempster had 101 steamers at the outbreak of war and lost forty-three of these, including twenty-five ships in 1917 alone. Four hundred and twenty employees died as a result of torpedo fire or sinking and, although the number of black casualties is impossible to quantify, they are likely to have been significant.[57]

African soldiers from Nigeria, The Gambia, Rhodesia (present day Zimbabwe), South Africa, Sierra Leone, Uganda, Nyasaland (now Malawi), Kenya and the Gold Coast (now Ghana), were recruited to serve in the war effort. Fifty five thousand African men served as soldiers, hundreds of thousands served in auxiliary roles as carriers and labourers; 10,000 Africans were killed or died while serving and 166 Africans were decorated. Overall, 60,000 black South Africans and 120,000 other Africans served in uniformed labour units. Many other Africans were recruited as labourers in African theatres of war. The British recruited over a million Africans to serve as labourers and porters, carrying heavy equipment for hundreds of miles across hot, arid conditions or wet, swampy land. The recruitment of African labour came at a huge price. Over one-fifth died of disease and starvation.

For those serving in the British and colonial forces, racism at the hands of commanding officers was a common experience. Included in the list from the African Christian Association are James Thomas and Davies Harrison, both 19 years of age and from Sierra Leone, who together signed up in October 1916 in Liverpool with the Coloured Labour Section of the Royal Engineers. They embarked for Mesopotamia where the section was to work as part of the Inland Water Transport Company. In January 1918, a formal complaint was sent to the Colonial Office on behalf of the Coloured Labour Section detailing the ill-treatment and conditions they were experiencing during the campaign. The men were underpaid – often not paid at all – and experienced racism at the hands of those in command. One striking note in the letter is that officers had threatened to shoot any man that complained to superiors about their situation. James was discharged from the forces in April 1918. On his discharge papers it stated that his unit was 'surplus' to requirements.[58]

A further and vital colonial contribution to the war effort took the form of thousands of workers who came to Britain to fill the labour shortage produced by increasing war-time demand and the gap left by British workers who had joined the forces. War-time migration from the colonies caused Liverpool's black community to grow appreciably. The local press claimed there were an additional 20,000 black people in the city, though it is generally agreed that this figure is hugely exaggerated. More realistic estimates are that at least 3,000 black men from West Africa and the West Indies who came to Liverpool at the outbreak of war increased the black population from approximately 2,000 to somewhere around 5,000.

Prior to the war, black workers were excluded from all but the lowest paid and most undesirable employment. With the onset of war, there was now well-paid work for black men to do and they were welcomed in munitions and chemical factories. Many others were employed in oil cake mills and sugar refineries. Black men now had access to employment opportunities that had previously been denied to them. Black seamen like Charles Wotten were welcomed into the merchant navy, as white seamen were required to serve in the Royal Navy. Similarly, opportunities opened up for white women who were brought into the workforce and were able to obtain factory work. However, the Lybro factory in Kensington, which supplied military uniforms and was Quaker-owned, was one of only a few firms that would employ black women.

Those who survived the horror of war, or who left their homelands to support the allies, were to be severely disappointed if they had hoped victory would bring respect, equality and freedom from colonial rule. The level of gratitude displayed by the British Government is exemplified by the fact that black servicemen were not allowed to participate in the victory march of 1919 in London that celebrated the end of the war, despite the large presence of white Australians, Canadians and South Africans. Just as racism was functionally necessary to the stability of imperial rule and war, it became critical in its aftermath, serving to divert the anger of an increasingly disillusioned white working class who expected a better standard of post-war living only to find their conditions worsening. The disillusionment felt by the black working class following World War I, and their experience of racism in Britain, was to have a profound impact on the emerging independence and anti-colonial movements across the empire. It was this anger, rather than the gratitude of the British establishment, that would move the colonies along the road toward independence.

Charles Wotten

Charles Wotten was a 24 year old ship's fireman from Bermuda. He was killed during the 1919 Race Riots by an angry mob, though the coroner recorded the murder as 'Death by drowning'.

A BBC commemorative plaque was erected in 2016 on the Queen's Dock, the sight of Charles Wotten's death. This plaque was not the first commemoration of him in Liverpool. Although no longer open, in 1974 members of the Liverpool 8 black community established a learning centre in his name.

Anderson Melville

Anderson James Melville was born in Grenada on 8th August 1893. He served in the 9th Battalion King's Own Royal Lancaster Regiment. This service regiment was part of what was known as 'Kitchener's Army', Anderson was one of almost half a million men who enlisted to serve during August and December 1914. He served in France and later in Solanki.

In December 1917, Anderson and Lillian Billington made their banns of marriage in St Stephen the Martyr's Church, but it was not until the 2nd of August 1918 that the couple married. At this time, he was 25 and she was 22 years old. It is interesting to note that between August 1918 and September 1920, Anderson is registered at the same address, 41 Bamber Street, suggesting that he had a permanent residence in the Toxteth area long before and after the race riots of 1919. After the war, Anderson continued to work on ships as a trimmer until at least the 1930s. His death was registered in south Liverpool in 1961.

Davies Harrison

Davies Ngba Harrison was born on 20th September 1894 in Sierra Leone. He enlisted on 3rd October 1916 in Liverpool into the 'Coloured Labour Section' of the Royal Engineers. Davies married Pauline Williams in the summer of 1927 in Liverpool. Pauline was born in Liverpool in 1901. In the 1911 Census, she is recorded as living with her mother, Eliza, and two siblings, George and Evelyn. The census also tells us that Pauline's parents had been married for sixteen years at that point and had had seven children, only three of which had survived. Their address was registered as 15 Tavistock Street, Dingle.

There are references to a number of children born in the late 1920s in Liverpool with the Harrison surname and Pauline's maiden name of Williams, although it is uncertain whether these relate to Davies and Pauline. Pauline's death was registered in Liverpool in 1969. No record of Davies' death has yet been found.

James Godonu

James Godonu was born in 1893 or 1894. He enlisted in the King's Liverpool Regiment on 2nd March 1916, but never served overseas. He was discharged on the 16th May 1919, and in September 1920 was recorded as living at 31 Nelson Street with his wife Florence and one child.

Joseph Annan

Joseph was born on August 5 1895. During World War I he served in the Merchant Marine Reserve as a greaser. Joseph married Mary Barnett in Liverpool in December 1919. By September 1920, Joseph was appealing to the African Christian Association for help and was residing at 3 Islington Row. In November 1920, Joseph left Liverpool for Canada. From Canadian shipping records we are told that Joseph was literate and claiming to be leaving Liverpool to settle permanently in Halifax with an aunt. When he left Britain, he was still married to Mary, as she is documented as his next of kin. The couple had no children. On September 7 1921, there is record of a J D Annan, with the same place of birth and birth year, leaving Liverpool on board the British African company Steamship, *The Appam*. This J D Annan is bound for the 'West Coast of Africa', and his occupation is recorded as 'agent'.

In November 1928 there is a record of a J Annan, again leaving Liverpool for the West Coast of Africa, this time on board an Elder Dempster ship.

Tom Oroma

Tom Oroma was born on 8th July 1893 in Warri, Nigeria. His father is recorded as Buku Oroma, a farmer. In 1915, he was medically examined at Birkenhead and it was determined that he would not be 'likely to become an efficient soldier', although there are no ailments recorded in the examination to warrant this decision. Tom served in the Warri Rifles, the Cheshire Regiment and the Merchant Navy during World War I. After the war, Tom settled and his occupation was recorded as 'sugarworker', indicating that he worked in one of Liverpool's numerous sugar factories. On September 1st 1917, Tom married Sara A Routledge, a nurse, who was born in Lochmaben, Dumfriesshire, Scotland in 1896/7. They married at the church of St Stephen the Martyr near Edge Lane. In the marriage banns, Tom's address is recorded as 17 Elizabeth Street and Sara's as 29 Boundry Place. Sara's father is recorded as Andrew Natt Carmichael, with his occupation as 'factory manager'.

In September 1920, Mr and Mrs Oroma were living at 51 Mount Pleasant.

Joseph Bynoe

Joseph Bynoe, a ship's fireman, was born in 1881 in Barbados. In 1907, he married Beatrice Whitacre in Liverpool. Beatrice was originally from Newport, South Wales. They had four children, three of whom, Gladys Mary, Keziah and Linzie, died in infancy. John Joseph (aka Barney), their oldest and surviving child, went on to serve in the Royal Artillery. In 1928, he married Anne Delves and they had one child, Thomas Joseph, a French polisher by trade, who in 1956 married Eileen Hayes. Thomas and Eileen had five children, Robert, John, Patricia, Eileen and Anne Marie, all of whom reside in Liverpool today.

Joseph's son and grandson,
John Joseph Bynoe (aka Barney) and Thomas Joseph Bynoe.

Archibald B Lyttle

Archibald Lyttle was born in 1896 in Freetown, Sierra Leone. He married Elizabeth Murphy in 1899. By 1920, Archibald and Elizabeth already had two children and went on to have a further nine. Their second child, Frances, born in 1919, married Charles Nimbley in 1943 and went on have four boys. One resides in Liverpool 8, while the others live in the wider Liverpool area. Their fourth child, Teresa, married Jose F dos Santos and had eight children. At least three of those children reside in the L8 area today. Sidney, Archibald's youngest child, married Patricia Jobson in 1961 and had two children, both of whom live in Liverpool today.

Kevin, Paul, Ronnie, and Graham Nimbley,
four of Archibald's grandchildren.

Paula Cargill, one of Archibald's grandchildren, with her children
(Archibald's great-grandchildren), Jamie and Amelia.

Riots & Revolt

The 1919 race riots are best understood in the context of the huge social unrest and working class dissatisfaction that was expressed, not only through intensifying racial tensions and violence, but in mass strikes, protests and calls for self-governance in colonised lands. One of the defining moments of the 20th century, the 1917 Russian Revolution, inspired workers across the world. In Europe, revolutions followed in Germany, Austria and Hungary, and mass Communist Parties grew. The Russian Revolution sent shock waves through the western ruling class, whose biggest fear was the 'red menace' of Bolshevism. The popular right-wing newspaper, *The British Citizen and Empire Worker*, using labour movement style rhetoric, battled with the Bolshevik bogeyman through cartoons, editorials and letters on a weekly basis throughout 1919. Interestingly, this paper and the group which produced it was directly funded by Viscount Milner, Secretary of the Colonial Office, with whom the Lord Mayor of Liverpool corresponded regarding the 'coloured labour' problem.[59]

In 1919, the political elite in Britain thought a Bolshevik style revolution was a real possibility: two thousand soldiers ordered to embark for France mutinied and went on strike; thousands of workers in Glasgow downed tools in demand of a 40-hour week; working days lost through strike action rose from six million in 1918 to almost thirty-five million in 1919.[60] In a move unimaginable today, the police force took strike action in protest at low pay. The police strike in Liverpool was the most solid, with over half of the force staying out on strike under threats of dismissal. Coming just weeks after the race riots, it resulted in further rioting and looting over a period of three days, which brought warships to the River Mersey, tanks to St George's Plateau and soldiers to restore order in the city.

Events in Russia influenced sections of the working class internationally, and this was accompanied by a high level of disillusionment among workers, both black and white, in post-war Britain. Lloyd George had promised 'a land fit for heroes', but instead the post-war economic slump caused high unemployment and a shortage of affordable housing. In this heightened atmosphere, the destructive power of war and the class tensions it had brutally exposed led to the emergence of disputes, which traditional ideas of military command and discipline failed to suppress.

Racial tensions began to emerge during the war years when increasingly politicised black servicemen agitated for an end to the racial discrimination that they had suffered, even as they were being maimed and killed in the line of duty. In December 1918, around 8,000 soldiers of the BWIR stationed in Taranto in Italy had been waiting for several months to be demobilised and given a passage home. Whilst there, they learned that their white British counterparts had been awarded a pay rise which was denied to the BWIR on the grounds that they were 'natives'. Angry that the pay rise did not extend to them, and further resentful at being ordered to wash the dirty linen and clean the toilets of British and Italian labourers, they mutinied for three days. The army responded by sentencing the leaders to up to five years' imprisonment, though one was imprisoned for twenty-one years and one was executed by firing squad. The Army later relented and black soldiers were awarded the same pay increase as their white counterparts. However, a white South African brigadier, brought in to take over the camp in Taranto and restore order, openly referred to the men as 'niggers' and refused to allow them to attend the cinema and participate in other recreational facilities. They eventually returned to the West Indies in September 1919, long after the white soldiers had been demobbed. As David Olusoga notes, 'the mistreatment of the men of BWIR starkly demonstrated to the people of the West Indies the reality of their place in the empire and exactly where they stood in the racial hierarchy'.[61]

In Liverpool during September 1918, an incident in Belmont Road Military Hospital a few weeks before the end of the war gave a portent of the racial tension to come. Around fifty of the two thousand or so wounded soldiers were black men. Relations between black and white soldiers had been good until the introduction into the hospital of white soldiers who had served in South Africa. Tensions quickly emerged, culminating in a pitched battle between some 400-500 white soldiers and fifty black servicemen. The black soldiers were attacked with crutches, sticks, pots, pans and kettles. Some white soldiers who had fought alongside these men tried to defend their comrades, many of them amputees, until the military police arrived and order was restored. The London press blamed the black soldiers, a pattern that was to be repeated throughout the period when racial violence occurred. A War Office enquiry found quite the opposite.[62]

Demobilisation resulted in thousands of returning soldiers and sailors being out of work. Black labour was now regarded as an impediment to work opportunities for white workers and a systematic campaign of discrimination, the imposition of a colour bar and the scapegoating of black labour and the black community as a whole took place. By March 1919, 2.5 million men and women had been discharged from the army alone; by December 1919 this number had reached 4 million.[63] It was from this now unemployed section of the population that those involved in the race riots that blighted Britain's port cities were drawn.

The social status of the different groups of merchant seamen proved crucial in an atmosphere of poverty, hardship and labour shortages. White British sailors, supported by their trade unions, demanded they be given first preference for work. Black British citizens, whether from commonwealth territories or British-born, asked to be treated equally with their white counterparts. Therefore, black sailors and white non-British sailors were in direct competition for the limited pool of jobs available after white British sailors were provided with the lion's share of job opportunities. Black and Asian sailors in British ports had difficulty in obtaining work. In Liverpool, the crews of four Blue Funnel Line ships at Birkenhead refused to sail under a Chinese chief steward. An Indian with four years' Royal Navy service, who had then worked on a river hopper, was told that white demobilised soldiers were to be employed first, even though his efficiency was praised. He found that Scandinavians were employed ahead of black labour.[64]

Joseph Hall's experience is common among black seafarers in post war Liverpool. Hall, who was residing at the Gordon Smith Institute for Seaman in Paradise Street, wrote to the Mayor on 31st May 1919:

I am distress, penniless and homeless and I am simply asking for assistance as I am a British subject. During the war it was alright for us coloured men but at present it is very bad. So if there is any way you can give me a helping hand I will be very much obliged. I am a married man with two children[65] (errors in original)

Hall was from Colon in Panama, and it seemed that he was requesting that the Mayor arrange with the Board of Trade a passage on a ship that was leaving for his home city in six days' time. On 3rd June 1919, a single sentence reply was sent to Joseph Hall from the Lord Mayor's Office stating that the Lord Mayor, 'regrets that it is not a matter in which he can interfere as he has no control over matters of this kind.'[66]

It was not just seafaring work from which black men were excluded as a result of white demobilisation. In factories, similar patterns of racial exclusion saw black workers dismissed from their jobs. Factory work that had been open to blacks at the start of the war, and that had paid well, began to impose colour bars. In the spring of 1919, 120 black workers, who had been employed for years in sugar refineries and oil cake mills, were sacked over the course of one week as white workers refused to work with them. The knock-on effect was profound. Unemployed black workers were now being evicted from their accommodation and living on credit, in poverty and hardship.[67]

On the 13th May 1919, Daniel T Aleifasukure Toummavah of the Liverpool Ethiopian Association met with the Lord Mayor of Liverpool, John Richie, to inform him of the plight of 600 black men, overwhelmingly British soldiers and sailors, who were unemployed, destitute and unable to find work on account of their race.[68] Many were wounded and disabled as a result of wartime activities and some were anxious to go home but could not afford to. In that month, the Lord Mayor had also received a delegation claiming to represent 5,000 unemployed white ex-servicemen who had complained

45

of the competition for jobs from black men in the city. The Lord Mayor outlined the concerns of both delegations to Viscount Milner, the Secretary of State for the Colonial Office, and made clear where his sympathies lay: 'One of the strong points made by this [white] deputation was the presence of black labour in our midst, a sentiment with which I thoroughly agree'. [69]

The letter also forewarned of the racial violence that was to erupt on the streets of Liverpool and suggested that paying each black person willing to be repatriated the sum of £5 would be in all parties' interest. The language used by the Lord Mayor is indicative of the attitude of the British post-war establishment, which defined a black presence as the source of the problem:

> If the government could repatriate these black men without delay it would not only be doing them a turn but relieve the irritation which the presence of these men causes to our men. Only the other night there was a fight between the two races, and matters are not likely to improve in in this direction as the position develops and probably grows worse. [70]

It was not until the violence turned into a full-blown riot that the Colonial Office considered this small financial incentive to repatriation. The Colonial Office's position in the month before the riots was revealed in an internal memo which suggested that 'a hint' should be given to the Lord Mayor that if Liverpool wanted to 'bribe' its colonial citizens to leave, then the city, rather than the Treasury, should foot the bill. [71] A repatriation scheme had been introduced in February of that year, though no financial allowances were made for black colonial workers. White colonial workers who sought repatriation were offered £5 from the onset, but as

Jenkinson observes: 'Black British subjects had to wait until they had been the victims of violent attack before this gratuity was offered them.'[72]

The violent disorder in Liverpool occurred in three phases. The first was in May 1919, with the second and third occurring in June of that year. Random attacks on black men peacefully going about their business occurred throughout May, and on 11th of that month, a black-run gambling house in Chestnut Street, off Mount Pleasant, was raided by police. Fourteen men and three white women were arrested. In court, the defendants claimed that the police arrived ready to fight. The major disturbances began on 4th June when John Johnson, a West Indian, was stabbed in the face by two Scandinavians because he refused to give them a cigarette. Johnson, as reported by the Head Constable, was taken to the Southern Royal Hospital with severe wounding.[73] The news spread quickly and a couple of nights later eight of Johnson's friends went to a pub at 1 Bailey Street in the area of 'Sailortown', that was, according to the police report, frequented by 'Scandinavians, Russians, Asiatics and negros'. A 'negro in navel uniform' is reported to have thrown beer over a group of Scandinavians who were then attacked by a number of black men armed with sticks, knives, razors and iron bars. In the process, they knocked a policeman unconscious. Five Scandinavians were taken to the hospital but only one was seriously hurt. The police reaction was to raid boarding houses used by black seamen. The black seamen dug in and defended themselves with weapons, including knives, razors and revolvers. One policeman was reportedly shot in the mouth and another in the neck, a third was slashed in the face and a fourth had his wrist broken.[74]

A mob had now formed, and Charles Wotten, a 24-year-old ship's fireman who had been discharged from the Merchant Navy in March 1919, ran from one of the raided houses in Pitt Street. He was pursued by two policemen and an angry 200-300 strong crowd throwing missiles at him. The policemen caught him at the edge of Queen's Dock. The mob tore Wotten from the police and threw him into the dock, where he was pelted with rocks as he swam. The *Liverpool Echo* reported that a detective tried to pull Wotten from the water, when a 'stone thrown from the middle of the crowd struck Wootton on the head and he sank'.[75] He died in the water, and later that evening his corpse was dredged from the dock. The police report on how Wotten died is strangely vague, given the amount of eye witnesses, including a large number of police officers. According to the Chief Constable, Wotten 'either jumped, was swept or thrown into the Dock and drowned, but it was too dark to actually say how he got there.'[76] It is incredible that in the subsequent inquest a verdict of 'Found drowned' was recorded and that, despite the heavy police presence, no arrests were made. As David Olusoga states, the most appropriate term to describe the murder of Charles Wotten was a lynching.[77]

During the next few days, there was mob rule on the streets of Liverpool. On the 8th June, three West African businessmen were stabbed and robbed in the street. On the 9th and 10th, mobs of well organised young men roamed the streets, their numbers variously estimated at between 2,000 and 10,000, 'savagely attacking and beating any negro they could find'.[78] *The Times* reported that in Toxteth Park thousands of people filled the streets seeking to attack any black people they could find.[79] A black man who held a good position on one of Liverpool's liners was dragged from a car, robbed of £175 and beaten, as was a black ex-serviceman who held three medals for war service. Homes and lodgings that were occupied by black people were being looted one after another and then set ablaze. Houses in Jackson Street, Dexter Street, Stanhope Street, Mill Street, Beaufort Street, Parliament Street and Chester Street were wrecked, ransacked, set on fire, or all three. The Elder Dempster hostel for black seamen, which held 300-400 men, was similarly wrecked, as was the David Lewis hostel for seafarers.

Police reports of the events presented to the Liverpool Watch Committee served to place the blame for the violence firmly upon the black community. The Head Constable's report denied any connection between the assault on John Johnson and the subsequent attack on the group of Scandinavians, portraying this incident as unprovoked violence by a group of 'West Indians'. The report paints a picture of black men involved as a serious criminal menace; 'a riot of negroes' armed with razors, sticks, iron bars and firearms, while the white crowd is described as consisting of mainly women and children. When the police were dispersing, the white crowd 'went quietly' while the 'negroes resisted arrest and assaulted the police'. The bravery of the police is emphasized, with one officer acting 'without waiting to consider his own risk'.[80] This account is hard to square with the Head Constable's subsequent description of the murder of Charles Wotten, who the police were unable to protect when the crowd 'came on the scene and commenced beating the negro'. Although 'P.C.s Higham and Atkinson did their best to prevent them[...] they were struck about the arms and body by the crowd with missiles intended for the negro.'[81]

Some contemporary historians have looked no further than police testimony for their understanding of the events that led to the killing of Charles Wotten. However, Jacqueline Jenkinson's in-depth analysis of 1919, using a variety of primary sources, locates the police portrayal of the black men as the aggressive instigators of the violence within the hostile relationship between the black community and the police.[82]

A letter from JA Devitt Martyn of the African Christian Association to the Lord Mayor gives some insight into the nature of this relationship:

> Thomas Thomas, residing at 2, Newton Street, was walking along Upper Parliament Street, when he was set on by six white men, beaten and robbed. NO ARRESTS WERE MADE .....in invariably every instance where this occurs, the police are usually "not there" or where there has been trouble between whites and blacks, or where our boys are assaulted and they instinctively endeavour to defend themselves, resulting in any arrests, the poor black man is as a rule the only victim. This we are asked to believe is "mere coincidence".[83]

The use of capitals and underlining would indicate a loss of patience by Martyn, who finishes on a note of sarcasm:

> In the meantime your pronouncement [assuring police protection for the black community] has left us breathing easier & our shuddering belief in the nation that is world famed for its "Sporting Instincts" & as exponents of Chivalry, Justice and fair play is considerably revived.[84]

Police attitudes to the black population are further illuminated in the subsequent discussion about the community's internment and repatriation, which will be examined in the next section.

Certainly, it would be wrong to portray the black community in Liverpool, or indeed the other seaports, as simply helpless victims. Many of those under attack had seen active service, regarded themselves as British citizens and expected the rights that such citizenship accorded. They were ready to defend themselves using whatever weaponry was at hand against the racist mob. Regardless of interpretation, what can be said with certainty about the events of June 1919 in Liverpool is that the police failed to control the streets where rioting took place and they were unable or unwilling to protect black people on the streets or in their homes. For several weeks in June, the black community were under siege from the mob. Men, women and children were forced to take refuge in the Ethiopian Hall and from there to seek protection in local fire stations and bridewells.[85] By 10th June, police, for their own safety, held over 700 black people, with more arriving regularly in the local bridewells and other places of sanctuary.

This was a situation that some white Liverpudlian's found unacceptable. On 13th June, a hand-written postcard was sent to the Lord Mayor by a PS Lyon of R Mathews & Co:

> Dear Sir, I understand that some of our coloured fellow citizens that are being sheltered in the various bridewells are without sustenance. Surely some of the wealthier members of the community could avert this disgrace. I am informed that some have fought for us in this war, that all at Lime Street are quiet and peaceable men. If you see fit to act in this matter I shall be pleased to give two guineas.[86]

The Presbyterian Church, though with rather more self-interest, also expressed sympathy when they heard, 'with sorrow and indignation' of the race riot 'which it regards as a blot upon the fair name of the city, and a danger to the Commonwealth at large'. It records its protest against 'a state of feeling which is opposed to the principals of the Christian religion, has led to grave crime, and is calculated to hinder the progress of Christ's kingdom at home and abroad.'[87] The reverend, based in Arundel Avenue, in what would have been a leafy suburb of the city, was clearly concerned that events would hamper the church's work converting the heathens to Christianity in the colonies. As shall be explored later, he was not alone in his concern regarding the global impact of the events which took place on the streets of Liverpool.

No such sympathetic feeling was expressed by the local newspapers, which sought to exacerbate an explosive situation and lay the blame for the violence firmly at the ransacked doors of the black community. The *Liverpool Courier* described residents of black neighbourhoods as 'pimps and bullies' and demanded 'the stern punishment of the black scoundrels.'[88] However, the local magistrate took a different view and condemned the white mob and accused them of '...making the name of Liverpool an abomination and disgrace to the rest of the country.'[89]

Much has been written on the causes of the 1919 race riots, with historians citing a range of contributory factors, including unemployment caused by the rapid rate of demobilisation and the resulting competition for jobs, alongside resentment towards interracial relationships and the prevalence of racism among the white working class. Academic opinion has broadly been divided between an understanding of the events as primarily economically motivated or principally to do with of race relations.

In *From Empire to Rialto*, Andrea Murphy asks, 'what was the threat actually from such relatively small numbers of discriminated black people?', given the size of the black population in relation to the thousands of white workers being demobilised every month. She makes the point that, 'there was no violent protest directed against the employment of Scandinavian and Russian seamen who were also competitors for "English jobs"'. She concludes, 'Only some tentative reasons can be offered for anti-black feeling in employment beyond endemic Liverpool racism.'[90]

While black workers would have been easily identifiable as 'foreign' and therefore easy targets, there is much evidence of hostility to other nationalities throughout the period. In June, the manager of the Employment Exchange in Liverpool reported to the Home Office that 'farmers would not or dare not, employ Chinese and Negroes on account of the bitter feeling that at present exists, and in the Ormskirk District, Irishmen are also unacceptable.'[91] While Murphy is correct that the numbers of black workers would have been relatively low in comparison to the entire labour force, the point remains that white workers believed black workers to be their direct economic competition and the cause of their unemployment. This belief was shaped by politicians, union officials and the press. In parliamentary debates during the period, the presence of 'alien' and 'foreign' workers is repeatedly discussed, and similarly cited as part of the scaremongering of Lloyd George's election campaign, which promised the eradication of 'aliens' from Britain. While the majority of black workers in the British seaports were British citizens, hostile rioters were unlikely to make this distinction.

To suggest that the rioting in 1919 rioting was due primarily to the prevalence of racism overlooks the fact that racism had been a feature of port cities long before the riots occurred. As Jenkinson argues:

White racialist thinking was too well-established a social phenomenon in twentieth century Britain for this to be anything more than a well-internalised mode of thought, called out into the open by a combination of economic and social pressures.[92]

Unemployment and the idea that black labour was a cause was clearly at the heart of escalating white hostility toward black workers. This understanding is evidenced by the delegations of black and white workers that visited John Richie, Mayor of Liverpool, in the months preceding the riots. That white workers reacted to a threat to their economic position, perceived or real, is clear from the letters from black men to the Lord Mayor in 1919 and 1920 recounting how they had been rendered unemployed because white workers refused to work alongside them. In September 1920, fifteen months after the rioting, the Lord Mayor, now Burton Willis Ellis, was still struggling to find a solution to this problem when writing to the Home Office regarding 350 men who have, 'been discharged from their employment from sugar factories and such places.'[93]

Jenkinson also identified the role of the Seaman's Union in the outbreak of the riots, arguing that its weakness and disorganisation meant that it was in no position to protect workers, black or white, from being rendered unemployed during the post-war slump in the shipping industry. This also meant that, 'when push came to pull the union representatives came down heavily on the side of their majority white membership, at the expense of Black British members.'[94] Certainly the NSFU was far from militant under the leadership of Havelock Wilson. After the outbreak of World War I Wilson began collaborating closely with the Admiralty and shipowners in support of the war effort, and in 1917 the Union provoked controversy by refusing to convey Labour Party Leader Arthur Henderson and

54

Ramsay MacDonald to a conference of socialist parties in Stockholm, which had been convened in the wake of the Russian Revolution to discuss the possibility of a peace policy. In 1921, the NSFU supported wage reductions imposed by the National Maritime Board. The NSFU was clearly not the vehicle to resist the economic hardship of seafarers in Liverpool in 1919.

Resentment towards black workers based on economic grounds, as many historians have argued, was undoubtedly compounded by the persistence of racist ideas and narratives, formulated in justification of the slave trade and then developed and refined in order to provide a justification for colonial expansion and dominance. As part of that belief system, a set of laws, rules and taboos existed, which condemned miscegenation and interracial relationships, though they were only applied to relationships between black men and white women. Sexual relationships between white men and indigenous girls and women were considered as almost a right by the British occupiers in the colonies.

Sir Ralph Williams, a former administrator in the Caribbean, exemplified the prevailing colonial view in a letter to *The Times*, in which he attempts to excuse the actions of white rioters:

> To almost every white man and woman who has lived a life among coloured races, intimate association between black men or coloured men and white women is a thing of horror...it is an instinctive certainty that sexual relations between white women and coloured men revolt our very nature....What blame to those white men who, seeing these conditions and loathing them resort to violence? [95]

The hypocrisy of this view is challenged in a letter to *The Times* published five days later from Felix Hercules, the Secretary of the Society of Peoples of African Origin, in which he draws attention to the situation in the colonies. There were, he claimed, 600,000 'half-caste' children in South Africa alone who were the results of unions between white men and indigenous women. Hercules continued by praising the white British women, 'who can see behind skin and behind superficial skin difference and recognize the man inside.' [96]

Fears surrounding the sexuality of black men and their relations with white women are a central feature of racist discourse from the pseudo- scientific racism of the 19th century to the lynching of 14-year-old Emmet Till in Mississippi in 1955. However, no evidence has been offered that such abhorrence to interracial relationships existed in the minds of the Liverpool rioters. Sexual jealousy however, which is something quite different, is offered as an explanation and again as a justification for the riots which occurred. The Head Constable, in his report to the Watch Committee, was keen to establish this justification in his opening:

> The Head Constable begs to report to the Watch Committee that for some time there has existed a feeling of animosity between the white and coloured populations in this city. This feeling has probably been engendered by the arrogant and overbearing conduct of the negro population towards the white and by the white women who live or cohabit with the black men boasting to the other women of the superior qualities of the negros as compared with those of the white men. [97]

Liverpool's Assistant Head constable was keen to proffer

the same cause for the rioting in his communication with the Under Secretary of State:

> The trouble has been caused by the citizens and the blacks, mainly on account of the blacks interfering with white women, capturing a portion of the labour market and West Indians having been demobilized here with plenty of cash, assuming an aggressive attitude.[98]

At the height of the violence in Liverpool both the local and national press were keen to excuse it on the basis that the prevalence of interracial relationships had understandably provoked the white rioters. *The Times* reported:

> ...during the war, the colony of coloured men in Liverpool, largely West Indians, increased until the men now number about 5,000. Many have married Liverpool women, and while it is admitted that some have made good husbands, the intermarriage of black men and white women, not to mention other relationships, has excited much feeling.[99]

The *Liverpool Courier* used the same justification, but with inflammatory language that was clearly designed to provoke anti-black feeling:

> One of the chief reasons of popular anger behind the present disturbances lies in the fact that the average negro is nearer the animal than is the average white man, and that there are women in Liverpool who have no self-respect..... It is quite true that many of the blacks in Liverpool are of a low type, that they insult and threaten respectable

women in the street and that they are invariably unpleasant and provocative.[100]

In addition, the *Courier* expressed the view that black men had somehow done well out of the war:

the fact that large numbers demobilised soldiers are unable to find work while the West Indian negroes, brought over to supply a labour shortage during the war, are able to 'swank' about in smart clothes on the proceeds of their industry ... to the annoyance of... the white man who regards him as part child, part animal and part savage.[101]

The *Manchester Guardian* continued in the same derogatory and inflammatory vein when it reported an interview with a serving police officer in Liverpool who stated:

The people here understand the negroes.... They know that most of them are only big children, who when they get money like to make a show....The negroes would not have been touched but for their relations with white women. This has caused the entire trouble.[102]

Although the subject of interracial relationships would often be met with opposition from newspaper articles and social and political commentators, they had long been a feature of port communities prior to 1919. But in 1919 the issue of interracial relationships, which had lain largely dormant, was used particularly by the media, to scapegoat black men and to sow fear, jealousy and hostility among working class white men who in large numbers had returned from their war efforts to be faced with little in the way of prospects. The media's role in using the issue of immigration to divert working class attention and anger away from those in power was as evident in 1919 as it is today. The black man stealing the white man's woman has startling parallels with the equation of black youth as the 'black mugger', as analysed as a constructed moral panic by Stuart Hall et al in the seminal *Policing the Crisis*.[103]

In the 1970s, a moral panic occurred in Britain around the idea of mugging, a concept which was imported from the US in the 1970s that tended to refer to being robbed by black men. Throughout this time, several newspapers repeatedly reported incidents of mugging. This moral panic, Hall argues, was built upon the idea of a collective fear of an 'enemy within'. He identified the idea of the black mugger as a scapegoat for other social ills of the period. Between 1945 and the late 1960s, Britain had prospered with full employment and improved living standards. However, the 1970s, like the years following World War I, brought about an economic decline, or as Hall describes it, a 'crisis of capitalism'. Again, with parallels to 1919, the 1970s brought wave after wave of strike action, civil unrest and the subsequent challenge to social order and the power of the state. Hall demonstrated that, by making the black mugger someone to fear, attention was deflected away from the failings of the State.

In 1919, local and national press, as well as local and national policy makers and authorities, were keen to highlight interracial relationships as the catalyst for the riots, rather than the more pertinent issue of unemployment. As with the portrayal of the black mugger, the police, the government and the media gave out one orchestrated message, in this case, that black men were a problem and their 'unnatural' sexual relationships with white women were an understandable cause for rioting. It is probable that sexual jealousies and resentment towards interracial relationships existed in 1919, but the extent to which this was a factor in the violence, or whether such claims, largely expressed by the police and the press as justification of the violence, were an attempt to manipulate public opinion, is hard to say. There appears to be no contemporary corroboration from the black or white workers involved. Ernest Marke, in his memoirs, makes no reference to interracial relationships being a cause of the riots. In fact, he was categorical in his assessment of the situation:

> I am not an intellectual; I left school too young. But whenever I am approached and asked by an intellectual or researcher, what, in my opinion, was the cause of the 1919 race riot I always say 'Unemployment!' [104]

In an interview for a BBC documentary made in 1994, Marke remained unequivocal on the cause of the riots. [105] Though Marke said he knew little of politics, he succinctly identified the ideological role of the black worker in the political and economic crisis of 1919:

> Unemployment usually leads to unrest and starvation. These in turn, make people look for a scapegoat. I know little about politics but I know one thing. Any state that allows itself to become stagnant with unemployment is courting disaster. The mobsters vented their feelings on the negro who happened to be the small majority and the underdog. If the negro hadn't been there the confusion might have been worse. Perhaps even revolution. [106]

1

12th June, 1919.

My dear Creedy,

Thank you for your letter about the Liverpool "niggers". I must say I am rather pleased by the subtlety of it. Having used these men in the Army and having then demobilized them in this unfortunate country, the Military Authorities plead no jurisdiction. However, my immediate object in writing is to say that we hear from the Chief Constable of Liverpool that General Edwards has agreed to take these blacks into a Camp if the War Office will give him the necessary authority, for which he has telegraphed. Would you kindly see that he has a telegram to-night giving him the necessary authority, as, though all is quiet at present, the keeping of the blacks throws a heavy strain on the Police Force.

Yours sincerely,

Sir Herbert Creedy, K.C.B.,C.V.O.

Letter from Edward Shortt, Home Secretary to Herbert Creedy, 12th June 1919, National Archive, HO 45 170

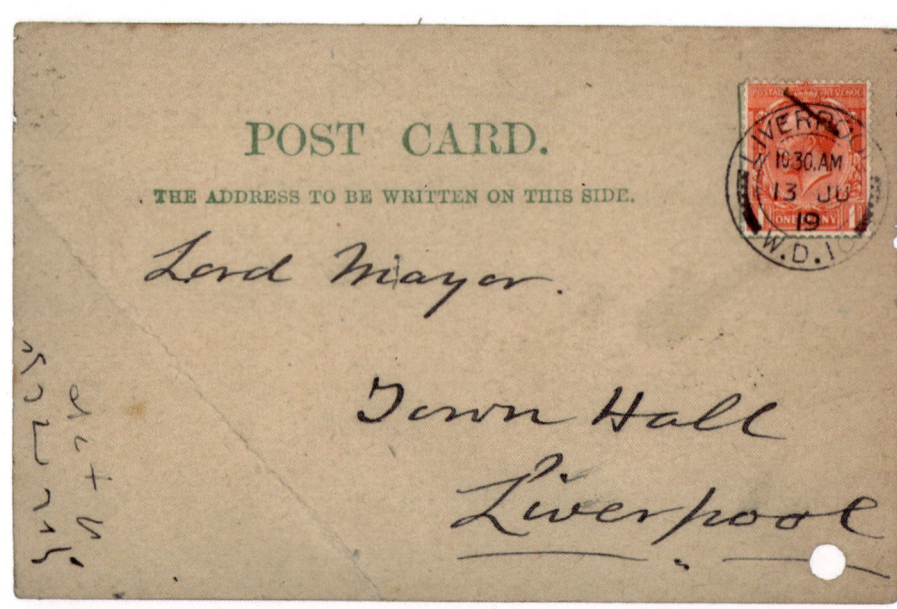

POST CARD.

. THE ADDRESS TO BE WRITTEN ON THIS SIDE.

Lord Mayor.

Town Hall

Liverpool

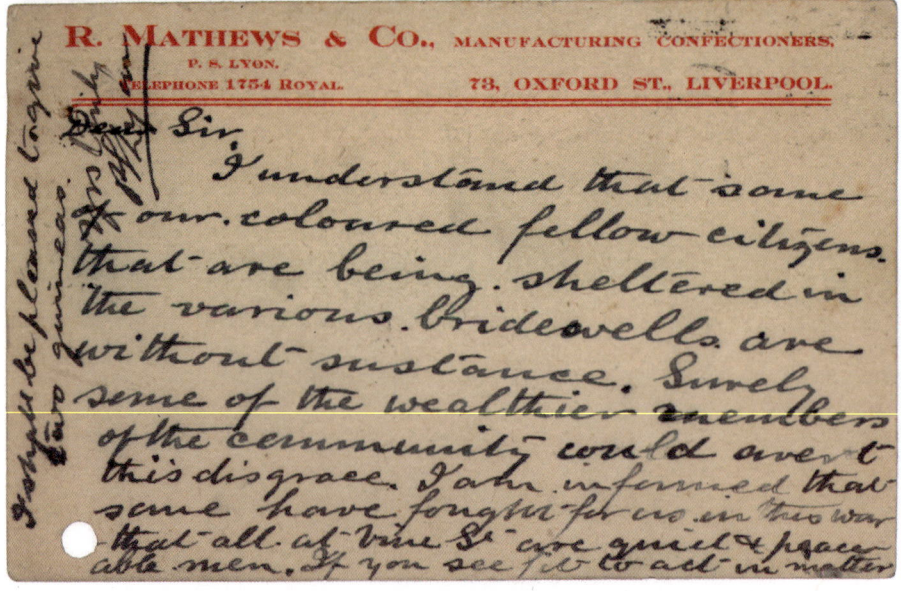

R. MATHEWS & CO., MANUFACTURING CONFECTIONERS,
P. S. LYON.
TELEPHONE 1754 ROYAL.   73, OXFORD ST., LIVERPOOL.

Dear Sir,
        I understand that some
of our coloured fellow citizens
that are being sheltered in
the various bridewells are
without sustance. Surely
some of the wealthier members
of the community could avert
this disgrace. I am informed that
some have fought for us in this war
that all at Vine St. are quiet & peace
able men. If you see fit to act in matter

Postcard from PS Lyon to the Lord Mayor of Liverpool,
2nd July 1919, Great War to Race Riots archive, Liverpool
Records Office

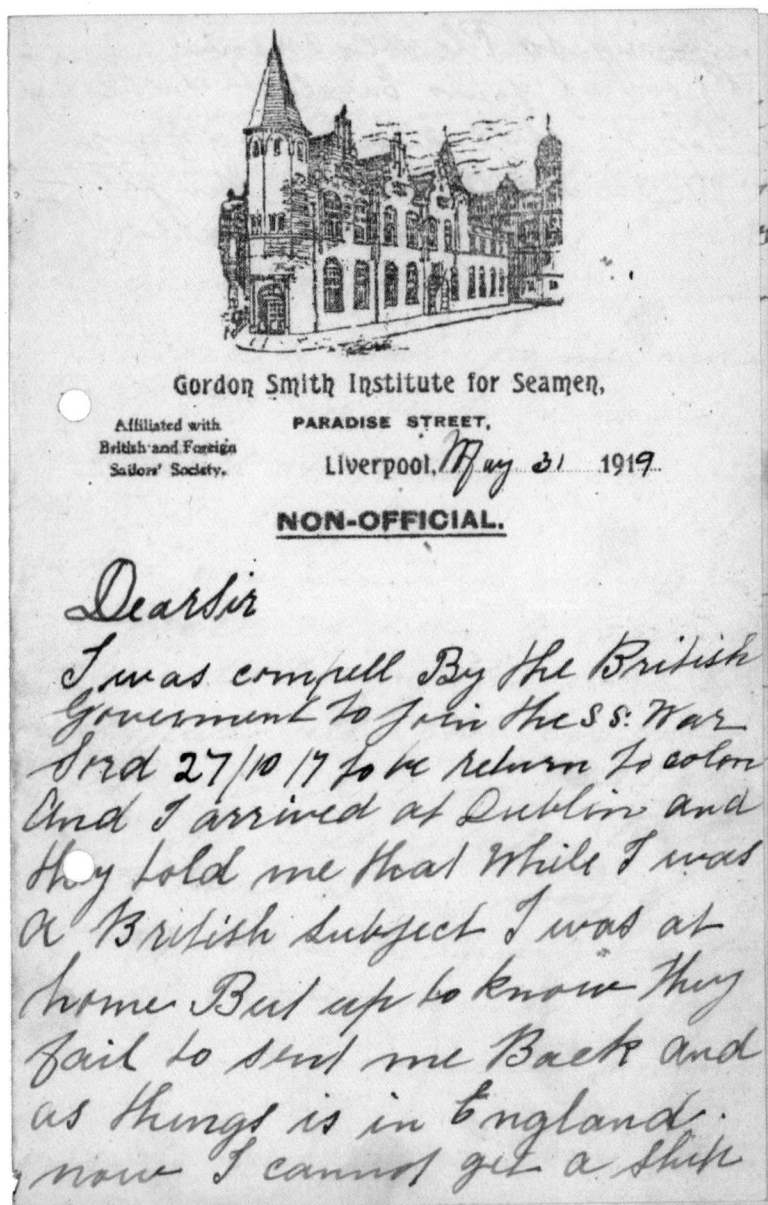

Gordon Smith Institute for Seamen,

Affiliated with
British and Foreign
Sailors' Society.

PARADISE STREET,

Liverpool, *May 31* 1919

NON-OFFICIAL.

Dear Sir

I was compell By the British
Government to join the S.S. War
Lord 27/10/17 to be return to colon
And I arrived at Dublin and
they told me that while I was
a British subject I was at
home But up to know they
fail to sent me Back and
as things is in England
now I cannot get a ship

Letter from Joseph Hall to the Lord Mayor of Liverpool, 31st May 1919, Great War to Race Riots archive, Liverpool Records Office

63

or anything Elce to do and
at Present there will be a ship
leaving for colon on Wednesday
the 4/6/19 and at Present I will
be very glad If you can interview
the Board of trade fro me and
See If they can Send me home
and Still ask to know I am
distress funnyless as homeless
and I am Simply asking you
assistance as I am a British
Subject during the war It
was quite allright for all
If us colourd men But at
Present it is affully Bad
So If there is any way of
giving me a helping hand
I will be very much Oblige
for I am a marraid man
with 2 children and you
must only judge how I am

64

living so Please answer me
By one of yours Earliest date my
Lord Still remaining your
Obedient British Subject
Joseph hall.

ETHIOPIAN HALL

(An Institute for the Advancement of the Coloured People in Great Britain & Ireland.)

ALEIFASAKURE TOUMMAVOH.
HON. SECRETARY.

43, Russell Street,
— Liverpool.

11. 3
Survey
the

Letterhead of Ethiopian Hall

66

Oct 30/q/. 20

Samuel Kelly

71 Soho street

Liverpool

To The Right Honarable Lord Mayor.

Dear Sir.

I am taking the Liberty of writing to you. Bemg a. Bretish West Jondian on Behalf of Myself an By Service Men. & a Few other by. Soldiers what is left in Liverpool we are not asking for Charity being true & Peaceable Britons but the Right

Letter from Samuel Kelly to the Lord Mayor of Liverpool, 30th September 1920, Great War to Race Riots archive, Liverpool Records Office

to Work. to Maintain
our ~~Wifes~~ Wives & Little
Children is Denied us.
what is to become of
us. When the Donation
of £ 1 . 0 . 0 Stops are
the Jaocent little one's
to Suffer on account of
us being Coloured Myself
& Other British West Indians
Gave our Services & Life's
during the War. & would
Gladly do So again
but its Work we want
& Work only So I beg
of you to. Please

try to use your great
influence on Behalf
of your coloured.
British Patriots I.
Remain
Yours
Sincerely. Samuel Kelly

x   x   x   x   x

Mr. Casely Hayford accepted the following alternative resolution which was seconded by Mr.E.J.P.Brown and carried unanimously:-

That this Council wishes to place on record its sympathy with the three Gold Coast British subjects viz:- Messrs C.R. Cathline, Jr., T.Jones Nelson and J.W.Nelson, who on June 10th last were the victims of personal violence and spoliation in the streets of Liverpool, its reprobation of this wanton attack, its regret that such an act should have occurred in England to mar the good-will which characterises the relations between the European and Native races in the Colony, its conviction that the incident was merely one of an unfortunate series having its origin in fortuitous and temporary circumstances caused by demobilization problems, and its confidence that His Majesty's Government and Municipal Authorities in the United Kingdom will take all possible steps to prevent any repetition of such outrages.

Further this Council requests that a copy of this resolution may be sent to the Secretary of State for the Colonies, the Lord Mayor of Liverpool, and to each of the above named gentlemen.

x   x   x   x   x

Extract from the minutes of a meeting of the Legislative
Council held at the public offices; Victoriaborg, Accra,
on Monday the 20th October 1919 at 10am. Great War to
Race Riots Archive, Liverpool Records Office

Lord Mayor
℅ Town Hall
Liverpool

Hilltop
Kirgfield Rd
Aintree
L.Pool
26. Oct. 1919

Dear Sir;

You may think it
very forward of me Writing
to you in this manner,
but I am doing it in the
right of my Comrades,
and also myself.

I came over to England
in 1915 with the first 500.
to land in this Country
from German South West
Africa, after 15 months hard
Work in the Desert.

Letter from A.F Oakley to the Lord Mayor of Liverpool,
26th October 1919, Great War to Race Riots Archive,
Liverpool Records Office.

2

In 1917. I won my Commission at menin Rd, getting my Transfer to the Royal Flying Corps, when I returned after the Armitice was Signed, I Threw up my Commision, and went to Russia, ao I saw troops where needed, now I. returned from Russia I am having a lot of Troubles with my money And the War office also the paymaster, here I am Waiting to Start Work at any menute of the day, I Cannot Start for the Simple reason

I cannot get my civilian clothes from the Sailor Shop.

I have only received up until the Sum of £ 9-10-1. My Credit alone is £68-10-0. Without 5 years gratuity.

I would be very much obliged if I could have a Private interview with you at your earliest date, in regards to the above. Hoping this will meet your most favourable Consideration.

I remain
Your Obedient Servant.
A. E. Oakley.

Partial list of

1. Coloured Men who served in the Great War. With Regiment (or Naval Unit) to which they were attached.

2. Coloured Single men who did not serve in the War (— but who were in the Merchant Marine)

3. Coloured men who have wife & children in the city.

N.B. All more or less seriously stranded in the City of Liverpool, as the result of an economic boycott launched against them in the name of the White Discharged Soldiers & Sailors & white Workers generally.

J Adeuitt Marlyn
Corr. Secty.
A.C.A
8 Nelson St
Liverpool
11/9/20

List supplied by the African Christian Association to the Lord Mayor of Liverpool, 11th September 1920 (b), Great War to Race Riots archive, Liverpool Records Office.

Coloured Ex-service Men Stranded in the city of Liverpool

1. J. D. Annan, Married, M.M.R 277465 Railwy, Greaser
   8 Islington Row (3)
2. J. Perris Married M.M.R 277459 Railwy Ord Seaman
   57 Bidder Street
3. T. Oroma Cheshire Regiment 26959, Married, 51 Pleasant
   St.
4. James Gordonu, married 3rd King's Liverpool 1132 50
   31 Nelson Street (Silver Badges)
5. A. J. Samuel 26 Middlesex (Die Hards) 4126, Married
   * (Silver Badges) under treatment receiving treatment allowance
   13 (very inadequate) has applied for repatriation. 31 Dove Street.
6. James Smith, single, labour Corps 681314, 52 Henry St
7. James Cole, Single, Royal Engineers 199749, 2 Eustace St
8. S. Brown Married, Civilian Prisoner of War in Germany
   14 Corkson Street.
9. James Thomas Royal Engineers, Single c/o 4 Hardy St. No 779
10. Davis Harrison R.E. 2 Newton Street
11. Thomas Williams M.M.R & Royal Engineers, 2 Newton St.
12. M. Williams, Married, Royal Engineers 199747, 17
    Moon Street,
13. S. Pratt, Single, Royal Engineers 122, 7 Mill Street
14. J Williams Single Royal Engineers 199796, 91 Victoria
    Terrace
15. H. Lewis, Served in the Navy, married, one child, 13 Parlia-
    ment Street

16. J. Johnson, Single Royal Engineers 420123 c/o 4 Hardy St.

17. Lloyd Pelly, Single, 2 Newton St Gold Coast Reg.

18. David, Single Royal Engineers 195, 123 Stanhope St.

19. Anderson Melville 9th Battalion King's Own Royal Lanc. 50355, 41 Bamber Street.

20. Tom Macauley, King's Liverpool Reg. 73161, Single 15 Parliament St.

21. ~~24776~~ J. Cole J.W.T. 526 Single 123 Stanhope St.

22. J. Lewis M.M.R Able Seaman 927469, Single 123 Stanhope Street

23. Daniel J.W.T & Royal Engineers 579, Single 123 Stanhope Street

24. Tom Johnson Royal Engineers ~~Married~~ 490, 123 Stanhope Street

25. Victor James M.M.R 927222, 6 May Terrace off High Gate St one leg amputed

26. Albert Elliott, Single Royal Engineers T.P.S 636 6 Dexter Street.

27. Joseph Wilson M.M.R, Single 6 Dexter St.

28. William Macpherson, Served in the Navy, Married 14 Corkson Street.

29. Himie Colombus M.M.R & Cameroon Campaign Brown Low Hill Work House, wife & 2 children Repatriation appealed for.

30. John Walker M.M.R. Stoker H.M.S Dunkirk, 30 Great Oxford St. Now in Brown Low Hill Infirmary.

31. Theophilus Flowers, 1st Batt Cheshire Regiment specially appeals for repatriation, now in Brown Low Hill Work House

3.

<u>Contd.</u>

32 Moses Williams Coloured Labours Section R.E. 199747
      C/o 4 Hardy Street.

33 Patrick Williams 2 W.7 R.E 26 Velten Street

                                        Jno Ballantyne
                                           Cor. Sect.

Smyle Men Men who did not serve in
in the War but who were in the Merchant
marine, factories etc.

1. Wm Ray c/o 4. Hardy Street
2. Fred Fergusson 2·3 White St off upper Pitt St
   presently patient in Brownlow Hill Infirmary.
3. Jack Johnson 113 Duke Street
4. Cyril Price 42 Great Newton Street
5. Fred Johnson 6 Hardy Street
6. Carl Bryant 6 Hardy Street
7. Thomas Thompson 115 Duke Street c/o 4 Hardy St.
8. Joseph Bill   10 Greek Street
9. Kossin Ayama 35 Great Orford St
10. Zac Kaupy 35 Great Orford St.
11. Bernard Lewis (Tom Peter)
12. Tom Dixon   } 62 Duckinfield St
13. Charlie Jones 30 Great Newton Street
14. W. Tu. Ray 5·9 Beaufort St
15. Tom Africa 113 Duke Street
16. W. Evans 5·9 Beaufort Street
17. Tom Walker 113 Duke St.
18. Thomas Johnson 113 Duke St.
19. Samuel S. Ross 48 Percy Street
20. Thomas Lewis 2 Newton Street
21. Martin Sampson 2 Newton Street
22. A. James 117 Warwick St

22	Joseph Thomas	59 Beaufort St
23	John Buckley	44 Heath St
24	T. Beckman	123 Stanhope Street
25	T Toby	59 Beaufort Street
26	T Bull	59 Beaufort Street
27	T Nelson	7 Mill Street
28	Tom Grey	123 Stanhope Street
~~24~~	~~Thomas King~~	~~123 Stanhope Street~~
29	Cecil Roach	35 Bumber St.
30	Tom James	27 Beaufort St.
31	William Dixon	2 Stanhope St
32	Joseph Jakul	29 Dickson St
~~33~~	~~Fred Fergusson~~	~~23 White St~~ 74 Upper Pitt St
~~34~~	~~Thomas Lewis~~	~~2 Nelson Street~~
~~33~~	~~T Nelson~~	~~7 Mill Street~~
33	Quasi	123 Stanhope Street
34	Sydney Duro	48 Nelson Street
35	William Johnson	} 2 Stanhope Street
36	John Davis	

Jas Martyn
Cor. Secy

Stranded Coloured Men.

Men who have wife & children in the city

1. J. D Annan 3 Islington Row
2. J Perris 57 Budder Street
3. T. Aroma 51 Pleasant Street
4. James Godoner, & one child 31 Nelson St.
5. A J Samuel 31 Dure St
6. S. Brown 14 Cookson St
7. M. Williams 17 Moon Street
8. He Lewis wife & child 13 Parliament Street
9. William Macpherson 14 Cookson Street
10. Kinie Colombus, wife & 2 children, Brown low Hill Work House
11. A. B Lyttle 77 Dottington Street, Everton & 2 children
12. Jim George 62 Duckingfield
13. Bernard J Lewis wife & 5 Children
14. William Vanterpool 29 Ashton St. 2 children
15. S. Wilkie 4 Hardy St.
16. M. Maxwell 6 Hardy St.
17. Joe Byron wife & child 20 Smithdown Lane
18. Sam Knox 2 Stanhope Street
19. M Williams 7 Moon St
20. J Hamburg 123 Stanhope St
21. G. Babbington Adeosi c/o 4 Hardy St 2 children
22. J. Lightburn 6 Crown Square
23. Samuel Kelly c/o 4 Hardy St
24. Tom Davis 57 Great Nelson Street.

Vincent Allantyn
Cor Secretary

Black Presence, Black Problem

The violence of 1919 caused a flurry of communications between the Lord Mayor's office in Liverpool and central government departments in which black presence, rather than white rioting, was defined as the problem. The removal of black workers from British society was generally agreed to be the solution to maintaining public order, though the mechanism for their removal was not so simple. Communications between the police in Liverpool and central government illustrate some confusion about the status of colonial workers who were not 'aliens' but who, regardless of the patriotic appeals to empire prior to the war, were now regarded as the unwanted 'other'. The victims of violence were labelled as the trouble causers, an attitude that persists in the policing and portrayal of black and Asian communities today.

From a government perspective though, the situation was tricky; perceived unfair treatment of colonial subjects, they feared, would impact on British rule in the colonies and, ultimately, on Britain's economic position in the world. Colonial administrators also feared reprisals against white settlers in the colonies where the exploitative nature of British rule was to some extent masked by the notion of the benevolent motherland. In the days following the riots, with black men and their families still under police protection in bridewells, Lionel Everett, the Assistant Head Constable, enquired of the Under Secretary of State for the Home Office:

If there is any power to intern them either on board ship or one of the Military Camps which is now vacant on the outskirts of the city and what steps he suggests removing the black population, some 2000, 3000 by compulsory repatriation or otherwise. I am confident that unless drastic and quick clearance is made, disturbance leading to loss of life will result. I am informed by Messrs. Elder, Dempster & Co that, if desired, they can fit up a ship to return 100 of them to West Africa next week.[107]

In a letter to Herbert Creedy, Under Secretary to the War Office, the Home Secretary Edward Shortt grants permission for internment while revealing his own, unrestrained racism and his amusement at the situation:

Thank you for your letter about the Liverpool "Niggers". I must say I am rather pleased by the subtlety of it. Having used these men in the army and having then demobilised them in this unfortunate country, the Military Authorities plead no jurisdiction. However, my immediate object in writing is to say that we hear from the Chief Constable of Liverpool that General Edwards has agreed to take these blacks into a camp if the war office will give him the necessary authority, for which he has telegrammed. Would you kindly see that he has a telegram to-night giving him the necessary authority, as, though all is quiet at present, the keeping of the blacks throws a heavy strain on the Police Force.[108]

Despite permission being granted and the *Daily Telegraph* reporting, 'Today an official from the Labour Ministry conferred with the Lord Mayor and Head Constable, and it was agreed to make arrangements for the internment of the negroes pending their repatriation,[109] on the 17th June the Head Constable reported that 720 men had returned to their homes and boarding houses.[110] Whilst the planned interment did not come to fruition for Liverpool and other seaports around the country, repatriation was still regarded as a viable solution to the 'coloured labour problem'.

Curiously, it was not just the British authorities who identified repatriation of colonial subjects as a solution to the problem of anti-black violence. On 12th June, Felix Hercules, on behalf of The Society of Peoples of African Origin, requested of Viscount Milner the repatriation of men that are 'signed off' or stranded, and even urges, 'that repatriation be compulsory in the case of men who came here during the war and for a specific purpose.'[111]

However, as Viscount Milner was forced to remind the police in Liverpool, any repatriation of British citizens had to be voluntary, though he added, it was considered 'desirable that all coloured men who are British citizens should be induced to return to their home country as quickly as possible.'[112] Clearly, the local and national governments were keen to be rid of black workers who were now surplus to requirements in a post-war economic downturn. The situation was quite delicate, however, as the British government needed to at least be seen to treat these men with some degree of justice for fear of repercussions in the colonies where there was increasing discontent with British rule. Viscount Milner outlines the fear of the British establishment at home and in colonial territories in his 'Memorandum on the Repatriation of Coloured Men':

These riots are serious enough from the point of view of the maintenance of order in this country, but they are even more serious in regard to their possible effect in the colonies... I have every reason to fear that when these men get back to their own colonies they might be tempted to revenge themselves on the white minorities there, unless we can do something to show that His Majesty's Government is not insensible to their complaints.[113]

A similar fear was expressed by the Legislative Council in Accra, the capital of the British Gold Coast, who, after the three West African businessmen were assaulted and robbed during the Liverpool riots, sent a resolution to the Lord Mayor expressing, 'regret that such an act should have occurred in England to mar the good-will which characterises the relations between the Europeans and Native Races in the Colony.'[114] The committee of the Africa Trade Section of the Liverpool Chamber of Commerce also expressed concern for the three businessmen, fearing implications for their trading relationship with West Africa: 'As this country is largely dependent on West Africa for edible products it's all the more unfortunate that Africans on business here should be involved in the troubles.'[115]

The question of compensation for the three visiting businessmen was raised in Parliament. The Colonial Office requested that the City of Liverpool be responsible for such a payment. The Town Clerk, responding on behalf of the Lord Mayor, took the opportunity to remind the Under Secretary of State of John Richie's request for £5 reparation monies back in May, suggesting that if the request had been granted the riots would not have occurred. Therefore, the Liverpool Finance Committee deemed the attack on the three West Africans a result of

Government inaction, concluding that the 'claims should be met out of imperial funds.'[116]

By the end of June 1919, a joint committee representing the Home Office, Colonial Office and Ministry of Labour, was now prepared to 'bribe' colonial citizens to leave, agreeing to offer the sum of approximately £5, plus £1 'crossing allowance' and free passage home. In the first instance, the scheme only applied to single men or married men with black wives, but by September 1919, as a result of the men's refusal to leave their families behind, provision for white wives and children was considered on a case by case basis. The debate around the inclusion of white wives was of course imbued with colonial racist thinking.[117]

Despite the offer of financial incentives, evidence clearly indicates that repatriation was not an attractive proposition to black workers in Liverpool. On 26th June, Inspector Burgess of Essex Street CID submitted a diligently compiled list to the Home Office of 437 'West African and West Indian negroes' living in the city. Burgess recognised that this was an incredibly low figure given that over 700 had recently been housed in bridewells. The reason behind this reduction, he explained, was 'an exodus of negros from the city to inland towns since the question of repatriation arose and those who have not left are probably in hiding.'[118] Burgess mentioned that the Board of Trade was offering £1 cash and a credit note of £1/8 shillings to West Indians who were willing to return, presumably in addition to the £5 mentioned in other government communications. No explanation is given as to why West Africans were not offered the additional amounts. In any case, the various sums would not even cover the debts accrued or the retrieval of pawned belongings. Burgess's detailed list indicated that a large proportion of the men were in debt to their landladies for sums ranging from a few shillings to as much as £8, with even greater sums owed to the pawnbrokers. The list gives a salutary insight into the conditions experienced by the men who, while out of work, were forced to borrow against their meagre belongings, usually clothing. One example is James Brown, a 28-year-old ship's fireman from Sierra Leone, resident in a hostel on Stanhope Street, who, after three months of unemployment and no recourse to 'out of work benefits', pawned his boots for nine shillings.[119] The list also illustrates how black workers were often dependent on the credit granted by landladies and landlords, many also black, to survive the hard times without work.

The inadequate financial allowances is one reason why the take up for repatriation was limited, not just in Liverpool but in other seaports. There were other factors preventing the men from returning home. Many were reluctant to return penniless. For some, the invitation was too hasty, with the immediacy of sailing leaving no time to plan for departure. Some who had agreed to return found the conditions on board to be substandard and refused to sail. The *Liverpool Echo* revealed the standard of accommodation on board the *Batanga*, which other reports indicate was not exceptional:

For his good accommodation provide them to sailed in we beg to draw the attention of the public to the course of our refused to sail as announce by the Ministry of Shipping. When we get on board Batanga, the Hatch was open, and we all asked to get (Down below), instead of cargo, where there is nothing provide for sitting nor sleeping for a sailing of 250 men on a voyage of 2 to 3 weeks. Though we black, but we are not sleeped in the Coal Bunck before we black. That's the Ministry of Shipping rewards to the negroes who has been risk there lives for him to get the praised the honour and the Title he received in this war.[120] (errors in original)

One very significant factor in the repatriation question was the issue of white wives. The official stance swung throughout the period and cases were often turned down which resulted in men refusing to leave their families behind. Even in cases of men with black wives who wished to be repatriated, the process was far from simple. Elisha Sterling, a Jamaican man, details how he had been informed by the police of a passage home for himself and his wife. On receiving this news, he gave up his position at J Bibby and Sons, an oil seed and soap refinery, only to find that when they reported to the Board of Trade the following morning, there was no accommodation on board for his wife. Aside from his employment situation, Elisha was distressed by the fact that his wife was confined to the house as she was insulted by people on the streets. His entreaty for assistance finishes with a rare contemporary insight into the psychological toll of racism on the victim: 'I believe if there is no help for us my wife will do some wrong to herself. Yours in haste Elisha Sterling.'[121] Another, perhaps overriding factor for both married and single men, was that the prospects facing them in their colonial nations would have been even harsher than those experienced in Liverpool. This perhaps explains why, in September 1920, the list from the African Christian Association of forty-seven men in abject poverty indicates that only three had applied to be repatriated.

While many men refused repatriation, a sizable number did leave under this government-sponsored scheme. There is no certainty about the numbers of men from Liverpool or indeed from the UK as a whole who were repatriated, but records indicate it was well over 1000 and perhaps nearer to 2000.[122] The incentivised repatriation scheme came to a close in November 1920 having done little to solve the problems of unemployment in Liverpool for black or white workers. The situation for many of those colonial citizens remained dire, as a letter written in September 1920 by an unidentified Indian man indicates. Housed in a Liverpool bridewell due to homelessness, he informed the Lord Mayor of how he had been laid off from Fairies sugar refinery and everywhere he went he was told that, due to government instructions, he cannot be employed:

> I don't want a thousand jobs I only want one and I like to know the reason why there are other nationalities working here so why can't I get a job this is fourth night I have been walking the streets and I never did any harm and I never was locked up the time the Indian men were locked up and I have got nobody to speak for me I hope this letter won't vext you as I have got nobody here to listen to me except God. (errors in the original)

His letter concludes: 'I feel I could throw myself into the river.'[123]

With repatriation providing only a partial solution to the perceived threat posed by black workers in Liverpool and the seaports of the UK, the authorities employed strategies to make it more difficult for black workers to gain entry and secure employment. In the wake of the riots, the Superintending Officer at the port of Liverpool introduced a new measure requiring black workers to provide documentary proof of British nationality before they could be paid off or sign on to a ship, a bureaucratic requirement that was impossible for thousands of seafarers born in British colonial Africa, the Caribbean, Middle East, India and Malaysia. This practice was subsequently incorporated into the Special Restriction (Coloured Seaman) Order in 1925 and applied throughout the country. Described as 'the white washing of Britain',[124] this order was the first form of immigration control designed to keep black people out. This racial bias was later manifested in the Immigration Acts of 1962, 1965, 1968 and 1971.

Official responses to the 'coloured labour problem' and the discourse around black workers in Liverpool and other seaports reveals an enduring attitude to Britain's black communities as a social problem, a problem which in 1919 needed to be 'expelled' from British society. Officialdom cared little for wartime sacrifices, the potential break up of families or the individual and collective experiences of poverty and racism. It was left largely to black people themselves to remind the authorities of their rights as British citizens and their contribution to the war effort. Black men in Liverpool and other seaports felt it necessary to wear their war medals as a sign of their service to the country's cause and spell out in their letters to the authorities how many of them had served their country with loyalty and distinction. Others asserted the principle of equal citizenship for all members of the empire, a principal that had been consistently propagated by the colonial authorities as a message of imperial commonality. It had been invoked particularly during the war recruitment drives that ultimately brought many of the men to Britain, and the sorry circumstances in which they found themselves in.

News of the race riots and the official responses travelled back to the colonies with repatriated men, who in the main returned home in poverty. Their feelings of resentment added to those of returning soldiers, particularly in the West Indian colonies, gave rise to increased anti-white feeling, with violent outbreaks occurring in Trinidad, Belize and Jamaica. Following a disturbance in Kingston in July 1919, in which the slogan 'kill the whites' was chanted, a confidential dispatch to the Colonial Office from the Acting Governor of Jamaica cites the treatment received by sailors in Cardiff and Liverpool as a factor.[125] A Colonial Office internal memo outlined the need for 'precautionary measures' due to an 'escalation in racial feeling accentuated by events in the U.K, & the U.S and to some extent by the grievances of the returned soldiers of the B.W.I.R.'[126]

The riots in Liverpool and other seaports were discussed globally by black leaders such as Marcus Garvey and Felix Hercules, the latter of whom the British authorities monitored closely during his speaking tour of the Caribbean.[127] Political and economic agitation and unrest were rising in the Indian sub-continent, South Africa and the Belgian Congo, as well as the West Indies. Anger at events in Liverpool was certainly a factor in this rising tide of global black consciousness.

Conclusion

The Great War to Race Riots archive of letters and documents represents an important find of great historical significance. It is a first-hand account of the British establishment's attitude toward and treatment of its own black British citizens, and provides a unique insight into the state of British race relations in the period immediately after the First World War. The archive demonstrates the lack of acknowledgement of their important contribution to the war effort and the role they played in furthering the interests of the nation. It also demonstrates how, in the face of racial discrimination, destitution, hostility and violence, the reaction of the authorities was not to protect the rights of black citizens but to propose their repatriation.

Liverpool's black community, like the city itself, was forged by the sea and its position as the empire's premier port. The city's wealth had been built firstly on the development of the slave trade, which allowed Liverpool to become Britain's foremost centre of the slave industry. Later, with the proceeds of slavery, Liverpool played a pivotal role in Britain's industrial revolution, with its port serving the coal, cotton, woollen and other industries in Lancashire, Yorkshire, Staffordshire and beyond. Black seafarers, attracted to the city by work opportunities and adventure, created a vibrant, thriving community made up of those from West Africa, the West Indies and the United States. The development of Britain as a colonial power also had the effect of attracting seafarers from its colonies as well as others from across the globe which led to Liverpool, and other ports cities, being instrumental in the creation of Britain's first and distinct black communities.

This community, located as it was in Liverpool's dockland area, or 'Sailortown', was part of a wider, more diverse and cosmopolitan world that helped to define Liverpool itself. The city's radicalism and exceptionalism emerged from this diversity, but its cosmopolitan nature is often romanticized as the events of 1919 aptly illustrate. The racist ideologies used to justify slavery and colonial expansion served to create the conditions for the violence and murder that occurred throughout 1919 across Britain and in Liverpool during that volatile and restless summer. The murder of Charles Wotten by a racist mob had its roots in the ideologies developed by those with vested interests in maintaining the trade in human cargo which were given credibility by an army of pseudo-scientists, doctors, psychologists and other assorted apologists for slavery and colonialism. These ideas had a devastating effect on the black community's existence. Such ideologies, coupled with the use by employers of African and West Indian seafarers as an army of cheap labour, helped to create their identity as outsiders who were stealing the jobs and livelihoods of white workers. The impact of demobilization at the end of the war and the correspondingly high levels of unemployment served to place black communities in a vulnerable position, as they became the convenient scapegoat for the economic ills of post-World War I Britain, which had unleashed mob violence, with demobilized soldiers and sailors at the head of these racist mobs. That the black community was forced to defend itself and take refuge for its own safety reflects the ferocity of the violence they encountered and the inability of the police and authorities to protect them. Such treatment was an indication of how the establishment would seek to manage race relations in the future. Their subsequent attempt to blame the community and attempt to repatriate the victims of violence indicated clearly where their priorities lay, and was be mirrored in later racist attacks such as the 1959 murder of Kelso Cochrane in Notting Hill and murder of Stephen Lawrence in South London in 1993.

The settlement in Liverpool by black seafarers and other workers during this period had a profound effect on the subsequent development of Liverpool's black community. They came as single men and chose to remain, even during the hardest of times. Like Archibald Lyttle, Joseph Bynoe, and Hubert Lewis, who are named in the archive, they married white women, and had diverse extended families, many of whom still reside in Liverpool and the surrounding areas today. Because of this pattern of black settlement, Liverpool's black population was much more of a mixed-heritage population in relation to other UK cities.[128] It was this heritage that has led historians and other academics to regard Liverpool's black community as 'exceptional.'

Liverpool's black experience compared with other cities, most notably London and Manchester, was also termed exceptional because it was not defined by the Windrush era of the late 1940s, when the government again welcomed its colonial citizens to fill its labour shortage. In 1948, the Commonwealth Act granted citizens from Commonwealth countries full rights of entry and settlement. This resulted in an estimated 172,000 British Caribbean-born people living in the UK by 1961.[129] The arrival of the *Empire Windrush* into Tilbury docks on 22nd June 1948 marked the symbolic beginning of post World War II immigration in the UK. The 490 passengers were the first of what was to be termed the 'Windrush generation'. They came to take up jobs in the NHS, the transport system, the Royal Mail and other sectors, but by comparison to the other major cities, Liverpool's post-war commonwealth immigration was a trickle. In October 1948, the *Orbita* docked in Liverpool with 180 workers from the Caribbean, followed three months later by the *Georgia*, carrying a further thirty-nine Jamaican arrivants.[130] This is not to suggest that black settlement had come to a halt by this time. Black seafarers continued to arrive and often to remain in Liverpool. This pattern continued until the decline of the shipping industry through the 70s and into the 80s, so that Liverpool's black community, like the city itself, continued to be defined by its relationship to the sea and its status as a port city.

As the infamous Fletcher Report of 1930 graphically illustrates, black presence in Liverpool continued to be viewed as a problem long after the race riots of 1919. *The Report on an Investigation into the Colour Problem in Liverpool and Other Ports* was commissioned by The Liverpool Association for the Welfare of Half-Caste Children, which was closely associated with the University of Liverpool and contained a glowing foreword by Professor Roxby, head of the Geography Department. Its sense of revulsion towards interracial relationships in 1919 now extended to the children produced by those relationships. According to Fletcher, mixed heritage children inherited the worst traits of both parents; lazy, morally and mentally deficient, their 'coloring and features' a 'handicap', and more prone to illness and disease. Mixed heritage children, it concluded, could never be accepted by mainstream society as their employment prospects were minimal and they would be shunned by both black and white. Fletcher and Roxby called for the reduction and strict regulation of black seafarers on British ships to eradicate the 'Colour Problem in Britain' and the 'Menace of Mixed Unions.'[131]

Though many of Fletcher's academic peers considered the report to be methodologically flawed and unworthy of serious consideration, it nevertheless served to stigmatize interracial relationships and shape public policy and official attitudes to those of mixed heritage. It embedded the pejorative term 'half-caste' into the British vocabulary and had a damaging impact upon race relations in Liverpool for decades.

In the inter-war years, Liverpool's black community had begun to move away from the dockland area into what was known as the Granby Triangle, though some families remained in the area, which became more commonly known as Chinatown. This movement into the Granby area was precipitated by the spaces left by the wealthy, who after World War I began to move into the suburbs, leaving behind large houses that were easily divided for multiple occupancy. The movement was accelerated when the Pitt Street and Upper Frederick Street areas were bombed during World War II. The black community settled in and around Granby Street, which became known for its shops selling commodities from around the world brought up from the docks and unavailable in any other part of town, and for providing support services for those newly arrived. It also became known for its black-owned night clubs, which played music from around the world. The Granby area retained the cosmopolitan nature of 'Sailortown', reflecting its seafaring heritage, with black, Asian, Arab and white families living side by side. In the 1980s and '90s, civil wars in the Yemen and Somalia brought new waves of immigrants to Granby, and immigration continues to be a feature of the area.

Negative and stereotypical attitudes followed the black community into Granby and the wider Liverpool 8 area. Views expressed by the police and others in their attempts to excuse the behaviour of white rioters in 1919, which were given academic credence by Fletcher in 1930, were still evident in the policing of that community throughout the twentieth century. In 1981, against a backdrop of severe economic recession and heavy, often violent policing, Liverpool 8 along with other inner-city areas, including Brixton in London and St Paul's in Bristol, exploded in anger. Liverpool 8 was by then home to the majority of the black community, though it remained a highly diverse area with a large white population. The 'Toxteth Riots' as they became known, brought national and international attention to Liverpool 8. These uprisings were a response to conditions which had existed in 1919 and which had become more acute, namely the racial bias of the police and disproportionate unemployment levels for black people. As in 1919, the black community was viewed by the authorities as having a propensity for criminality and violence. The approach to policing the community was one that ran from the top down, as revealed by Chief Constable Ken Oxford's interview in the *Listener* magazine in 1979 in which he rejected the claim that his force was racist but argued that his officers were, 'the first to define the problem of half-castes in Liverpool.' His characterization of Liverpool's mixed heritage population could almost be lifted verbatim from the Fletcher report:

> Many are the products of liaisons between Black seamen and white prostitutes in Liverpool 8, the red-light district. Naturally they grow up without any kind of recognisable home life. Worse still, after they have done the rounds of homes and institutions they gradually realise that they are nothing. The Negroes will not accept them as Blacks, and whites just assume they are coloureds.

As a result, the half-caste community of Merseyside – or more particularly Liverpool – is well outside recognised society.' [132]

Such views allowed Oxford to depoliticise the events and blame them on, 'a crowd of black hooligans intent on making life unbearable and indulging in criminal activities'. [133] Over half of those arrested were white, but due to such statements the events in Liverpool and other inner-city areas in 1981 have often been termed 'race riots'. In fact, they were a multicultural response to economic and social issues including the marginalisation of both black and white youth within those inner-city areas, rather than the traditional notion of a race riot, whereby blacks and white are directly opposed to each other. The reality of racist policing methods was established and highlighted by the community of Liverpool 8 and organisations such as the Liverpool 8 Defence Committee that represented the community. Police Racism was subsequently documented in the Scarman report, which in part exonerated those involved in the uprisings from the charges of mindless criminality. [134] However, the 'Toxteth Riots' continued to define popular public perceptions of the area and of Liverpool's black community for decades to come.

While there are a number of similarities between 1919 and 1981, there are clearly a number of significant and crucial differences. In 1981, the community fought back against institutional rather than popular racism and, in doing so, they were supported by white people within that community who also had grievances against the establishment. Their anger was not diverted towards a black scapegoat but most definitely directed at the police as the agents of the establishment.

The discourse on immigration continues to provide

racialized moral panics, particularly in the reporting of paedophile gangs characterised as being predominantly Asian and the terrorist threat from Islamic extremists as being a Muslim problem. In an increasing climate of hostility Europe has closed its borders, and those fleeing war, starvation and persecution are forced to take perilous sea crossings with thousands drowning each month. The momentary collective outrage at the photograph of toddler, Alan Kurdi,[135] drowned and washed up on a Turkish beach, was quickly eclipsed by news headlines that screamed of 'swarms' of refugees and newspaper editorials demanding, among other measures, dental checks on migrant children to determine their age.[136]

Direct parallels can be drawn between the spurious claims of 1919, which led to the race riots, and the continuing racist discourse today, which claims that immigrants are taking British jobs and are responsible for the strain on public services and the lack of decent and affordable housing. Such claims, as in 1919, serve to divert attention from the government's economic policies. However, there is an important divergence. In 1919 it was left to the black community itself to mount their own defense when they came under attack. In recent years, a more unified opposition involving black and Asian communities, trade unions, the organized left, and white anti-racists has provided strong and effective opposition to racist activity. This was perhaps best illustrated in 2015 and 2017 when far right groups were prevented from marching through Liverpool due to the scale of counter protests and the determination of the city's population to protect its historically multicultural identity. Hopefully, this sense of 'Scouse pride' in a city built on immigration, will continue to be a key feature of its exceptionalism.

Notes

Introduction

[1] List supplied by the African Christian Association to the Lord Mayor of Liverpool 11th September 1920 (b), Great War to Race Riots (GWRRA), Liverpool Records Office (LRO).

[2] Charles Wotten's name was spelt in variety of ways in police and newspaper reports following his murder. 'Wotten' is the spelling on his naval identity card, completed while he was alive, and so would seem the most reliable.

[3] Marke, Ernest, *Old Man Trouble*, (London: Weidenfeld and Nicolson, 1975).

[4] John Bull is a national personification of the United Kingdom in general and England in particular. The figure came to be associated with patriotism, and then jingoistic racism. It is still a term used in modern day Liverpool to denote a racist white man.

The Formation of Liverpool's Black Community

[5] Fryer, Peter, *Staying Power: The History of Black People in Britain* (London: Pluto, 1984), p34.

[6] Ibid, p34.

[7] Ibid, p35.

[8] Ibid, p37.

[9] Rediker, Marcus, *The Slave Ship: A Human History*, (London: John Murray, 2007), p224.

[10] Fryer, p54-55.

[11] Rediker, p224.

[12] Fryer, p191-2.

[13] The National Archives, *Black Presence*, 'Introduction: Arriving In Britain', http://www.nationalarchives.gov.uk/pathways/blackhistory/intro/intro.html

[14] Walvin, James, *England, Slaves and Freedom 1776-1838*, (London: Macmillan, 1986), p6.

[15] Equiano, Olaudah, *The Interesting Narrative of the Life of Olaudah Equiano* (1789) (Ontario: Broadview 2016).

[16] Olusoga, David, *Black and British: A Forgotten History*, (Kindle Edition: Pan, 2016), p 6126 - 6497.

[17] Fryer, p210-11.

[18] Rediker, p323.

[19] Walvin, p260.

[20] For example, James Walvin, Peter Fryer, Walter Rodney.

[21] Fryer, p134.

[22] Ibid, p134.

Liverpool, Gateway to Empire

[23] Jones, Ernest *The New World* (1851) cited in Rennie, Simon, *The Poetry of Ernest Jones, Myth, Song, and the 'Mighty Mind'* (Cambridge: Routledge, 2016).

[24] Newsinger, John, *The Blood Never Dries, A People's History of the British Empire* (London: Bookmarks, 2006).

[25] Gilroy, Paul, *Postcolonial Melancholia* (Wellek Library Lectures), (New York: Columbia University Press, 2008).

[26] YouGov160118 'British Empire,' 18th January 2016. 44% of 1733 of respondents were proud of Britain's history of colonialism; 21% regretted that it happened; 23% held neither view. 43% of respondents said the British Empire was good, while only 19% said it was bad. 25% cent said that it was neither.

[27] Loomba, Anai, *Colonialism/Post Colonialism* (London: Routledge, 2010), p9.

[28] Hunt, Tristram, *Ten Cities That Made an Empire* (Harmondsworth: Penguin, 2014), p395.

[29] University College London, *Legacies of British Slave Ownership*, London, https://www.ucl.ac.uk/lbs/.

[30] Guyana.net. 'The Bookers Empire', http://www.guyana.org/features/guyanastory/chapter112.html.

[31] Walvin, p47.

[32] Nassy Brown, Jacqueline, *Dropping Anchor, Setting Sail: Geographies of Race in Black Liverpool* (Princeton: Princeton University Press, 1994), p19.

[33] Ibid.

[34] Belchem John, *Before the Windrush: Race Relations in Twentieth-Century Liverpool*, (Liverpool: Liverpool University Press, 2014), p42

[35] Ibid, p22.

[36] Walvin, p49.

[37] Jenkinson, Jaqueline, *The 1919 Race Riots in Britain: Their background and Consequences*, (For the Degree of Philosophy), (University of Edinburgh, 1987), p207.

[38] Benton Gregor, & Edmund Gomez, *The Chinese in Britain 1800-Present, Economy, Transnationalism, and Identity*, (Basingstoke: Palgrave Macmillan, 2008), p69.

[39] Belchem, 2014, p26.

[40] Belchem, John, *Irish, Catholic and Scouse: The History of the Liverpool-Irish, 1800-1939*, (Oxford: Oxford University Press, 2007), p7.

Defending the Motherland

[41] Costello, Ray, *Black Tommies: British Soldiers of African Descent in the First World War*, (Liverpool: Liverpool University Press, 2015), 2015, p1.

[42] Ahmed, Talat, 'The British Empire and the First World War: The Colonial Experience', *International Socialist Journal* 152 http://isj.org.uk/the-british-empire-and-the-first-world-war-the-colonial-experience/.

[43] Olusoga, p7495.

[44] GWRRA, (LRO).

[45] Ahmed.

[46] Ibid.

[47] Ibid.

[48] Costello, 2015, p18.

[49] Hamilton Johnson, Harry, *The Black Man's Part in the War: An Account of the Dark-Skinned Population of the British Empire*, (1917) (London: Kessinger, 2016), p8-9.

[50] Spry Rush, Anne, *Bonds of Empire: West Indians and Britishness from Victoria to Decolonization*, (Oxford: Oxford University Press, 2011), p121.

[51] Bourne, Stephen, *Black Poppies: Britain's Black Community and the Great War* (Stroud: The History Press, 2014), p68-69.

[52] List supplied by the African Christian Association to the Lord Mayor of Liverpool, 11th September 1920 (b), GWRRA, (LRO).

[53] Costello, 2015, p26.

[54] List supplied by the African Christian Association to the Lord Mayor of Liverpool, 11th September 1920 (b), GWRRA, (LRO).

[55] Costello, 2015, p93.

[56] Centenary News, *First World War 1914-1918*, http://www.centenarynews.com/article?id=3262.

[57] Elder Dempster, *The History of Elder Dempster* http://www.rakaia.co.uk/assets/elder-dempster-history-summary.pdf.

[58] Letter from Mesopotamia Expeditionary Force, Royal Engineers Coloured Section to the Colonial Office, 29th January 1918, reproduced in Costello, 2015, p85.

Riots & Revolt

[59] GWRRA, (LRO).

[60] Rosenberg, Chanie, *Britain on the Brink of Revolution, 1919* (London: Bookmarks, 1987), p7-9.

[61] Olusoga, p7971.

[62] Fryer, p297.

[63] Jenkinson, Jaqueline, *Black 1919: Riots, Racism and Resistance in Imperial Britain* (Liverpool: Liverpool University Press, 2009), p39.

[64] May, Roy & Robin Cohen, 'The Interaction Between Race and Colonialism: A Case Study of the Liverpool Race Riots of 1919', *Race and Class*, (1974) 16, 2, p121.

[65] Letter from Joseph Hall to the Lord Mayor 31st May 1919, GWRRA, (LRO).

[66] Letter from Town Hall Clerk to Joseph Hall, 3rd June 1919, GWRRA, (LRO).

[67] *Liverpool Courier*, 11th June 1919, quoted in Fryer, p299.

[68] Fryer, p299-300.

[69] Letter from the Lord Mayor to the Secretary of the Colonial office, 13th May 1919, GWRRA, (LRO).

[70] Ibid.

[71] Internal Memorandum, Home Office, 29th May 1919, National Archives (NA) CO 323 819.

[72] Jenkinson, 1987, p185.

[73] Report to the Head Constable on the Race Riots to the Liverpool Watch Committee, 24th June 2019, (LRO).

[74] The shooting of a police officer may seem incredible by today's standards but it was not until 1919 that legislation began to be brought in to regulate and licence the ownership of hand guns. It was common that soldiers returned from the war with their weapons.

[75] *Liverpool Echo*, 10th June 1919, cited in Jenkinson, 1987, p171.

[76] Report to the Head Constable on the Race Riots to the Liverpool Watch Committee, 24th June 2019, (LRO).

[77] Olusoga, p8010.

[78] Report to the Head Constable on the Race Riots to the Liverpool Watch Committee, 24th June 2019, (LRO).

[79] Fryer, p301.

[80] Report to the Head Constable on the Race Riots to the Liverpool Watch Committee, 24th June 2019, (LRO).

[81] Ibid.

[82] Jenkinson, 2009 p131-155.

[83] Letter from JA Devitt Martyn, Secretary of the African Christian Association, Lord Mayor of Liverpool, 7th October 1920, GWRRA, (LRO).

[84] Ibid.

[85] Term meaning 'police station'.

[86] Postcard from PS Lyon to The Lord Mayor, 13th June 1919, GWRRA, (LRO).

[87] Letter from The Presbyterian Church to the Lord Mayor of Liverpool, 2nd July 1919, GWRRA, (LRO).

[88] *Liverpool Courier*, 11th June 1919, quoted in Fryer, p302-3.

[89] Fryer, p303.

[90] Murphy, Andrea, *From Empire to Rialto: Racism and Reaction In Liverpool 1918-1948* (Liverpool: Liverpool University Press, 1995), p57.

[91] Letter from Office of the Superintending Alien Officer to HM Inspector, 11th June 1919, NA, HO 45 11017 7.

[92] Jenkinson, 1987, p3.

[93] Letter from Lord Mayor to H Maxwell of the Home Office, 6th September 1920, GWRRA, (LRO).

[94] Jenkinson, 1987, p270.

[95] Letter to *The Times*, 14th June 1919, quoted in Fryer, p311.

[96] Letter to *The Times*, 18th June 1919, quoted in Fryer, p311.

[97] Report of the Head Constable to the Watch Committee, 24th June 1919, (LRO).

[98] Letter from Lionel Everett, Assistant Head Constable to the Under Secretary of State, 10th June 2019. NA, HO45 11017 2.

[99] *The Times*, 10th June 1919, quoted in Jenkinson, 1987, p164.

[100] *Liverpool Courier*, 11th June 1919, quoted in Fryer, p302.

[101] Ibid.

[102] *Manchester Guardian*, 12th June 1919, Fryer, p302.

[103] Hall, Stuart, Chas Critcher, Tony Jefferson, John Clarke, Brian Roberts, *Policing the Crisis: Mugging, The State, and Law and Order,* (London & Basingstoke: Macmillan, 1978).

[104] Marke, p31.

[105] BBC *Forbidden Riots* (1994) https://www.youtube.com/watch?v=6Pc-SVZhyG0.

[106] Marke, p32.

Black Presence, Black Problem

[107] Telegram from Lionel Everett, Assistant Head Constable to the Under Secretary of State, June 1919, NA, HO 45 11017.

[108] Letter from Edward Shortt, Home Secretary to Herbert Creedy, 12th June 1919 NA, HO 45 170.

[109] Rowe, Michael, 'Sex Race and Riot in Liverpool 1919', *Immigrants and Minorities Historical Studies in Ethnicity, Migration and Diaspora,* 19, 2 (2000), p62.

[110] Handwritten note from the Head Constable, 17th June 1919, NA, HO 45 1017.

[111] Letter from Society of Peoples of African Origin to Secretary of State for the Colonies, 12 June 1919, NA, CO 323 814.

[112] Letter from Home Office Civil Servant, to Liverpool's Chief Constable, 18th June 1919, NA, HO45 11017.

[113] Memorandum on the Repatriation of Coloured Men, 23rd June 1919, NA, CO 323/814-283.

[114] Extract from minutes from Legislative Council of Victoriaborg, Accra, 20th October 1919, GWRRA, (LRO).

[115] Liverpool Watch Committee Minutes, 17th June 1919, (LRO).

[116] Letter from Edward R. Pickmere Esq, Town Clerk Liverpool to the Under Secretary of State, 7th October 1919, GWRRA, (LRO).

[117] Jenkinson, 2009, p170-3.

[118] Report from Inspector Burgess, CIB to Home Office, 26th June 1919, NA, HO 45 11017, p1.

[119] Ibid, p30.

[120] *Liverpool Echo,* 19th June 1919, quoted in Jenkinson, 1987, p135.

[121] Letter from Elisha Sterling to Lord Mayor of Liverpool, 2nd July 1919, GWRRA, (LRO).

[122] Jenkinson, 1987, p191.

[123] Unsigned letter to Lord Mayor of Liverpool, 28th September 1920, GWRRA, (LRO).

[124] Paul, Kathleen, *Whitewashing Britain: Race and citizenship in the Post War Era*, (NY: Cornell University Press 1997), quoted in Belchem, p56.

[125] Confidential dispatch from Acting Governor Johnstone of Jamaica to CO, 14th August 1919, NA, CO 137/733.

[126] Colonial Office internal memorandum, 3rd October 1919, NA, CO 318 350.

[127] Letter from Johnstone, Acting Governor of Jamaica, to the Colonial Office, 25 July 1919, NA, CO 318/349.

Conclusion

[128] According to the 2011 Census, London has a total BME population of 55.1, 5% of which identify as 'Mixed'. Liverpool has a total BME population of 13.8% of which 2.5% identify as mixed. London's 'mixed' population is therefore 9% of its BME population, while Liverpool's is 18%. While census data is not wholly accurate and is generally regarded as an underestimation of the size of BME populations, it does present a broad picture.

[129] Alexander, Saffron, 'Windrush Generation:' 'They thought we should be planting bananas', *The Times*, 22nd June 2015.

[130] Fryer, p372.

[131] See Christian, Mark, 'The Fletcher Report 1930: A Historical Case Study of Contested Black Mixed Heritage Britishness', *Journal of Historical Sociology* Vol. 21 No. 2/3 June/September 2008 ISSN 0952-1909.

[132] Interview with Ken Oxford in the *Listener* Magazine, (1979), cited in Frost, Diane & Richard Phillips, 'The 2011 Summer Riots: Learning from History -Remembering '81', *Sociological Research Online*, 17 (3) 19, <http://www.socresonline.org.uk/17/3/19.html>10.5153/sro.2718.

[133] Ibid.

[134] Lord Scarman, *The Scarman Report: The Brixton Disorders 10-12 April 1981* (London, Pelican, 1982).

[135] Previously named as Aylan Kurdi in press reports. Wikipedia *The Death of Alan Kurdi*, https://en.wikipedia.org/wiki/Death_of_Alan_Kurdi.

[136] Smith, Reiss, How could the Home Office age check Calais migrant 'children' from dental records? *Daily Express*, 19th October, 2016.

Bibliography

Books

Belchem John, *Before the Windrush: Race Relations in Twentieth-Century Liverpool*, (Liverpool: Liverpool University Press, 2014).

Belchem, John, Irish, Catholic and Scouse: *The History of the Liverpool-Irish*, 1800-1939 (Oxford: Oxford University Press, 2007).

Benton Gregor & Edmund Gomez, *The Chinese in Britain, 1800-Present: Economy, Transnationalism, Identity*, (Basingstoke: Palgrave Macmillan, 2008).

Bourne, Stephen, *Black Poppies: Britain's Black Community and the Great War*, (Stroud: The History Press, 2014).

Costello, Ray, *Black Salt: Seafarers of African Descent on British Ships*, (Liverpool: Liverpool University Press, 2014).

Costello, Ray, *Black Tommies: British Soldiers of African Descent in the First World War*, (Liverpool: Liverpool University Press, 2015).

Equiano, Olaudah, *The Interesting Narrative of the Life of Olaudah Equiano* (1789), (Ontario: Broadview 2016).

Fryer, Peter, *Staying Power: The History of Black People in Britain*, (London: Pluto Press, 1984).

Gilroy, Paul, *Postcolonial Melancholia* (Wellek Library Lectures), (New York: Columbia University Press, 2008).

Hall, Stuart, Chas Critcher, Tony Jefferson, John Clarke, & Brian Roberts, *Policing the Crisis: Mugging, The State, and Law and Order*, (London & Basingstoke: Macmillan, 1978).

Hamilton Johnson, Harry, *The Black Man's Part in the War: An Account of the Dark-Skinned Population of the British Empire* (1917), (London: Kessinger, 2016).

Hunt, Tristram, *Ten Cities That Made an Empire* (Harmondsworth: Penguin, 2014).

Jenkinson, Jacqueline, *Black 1919: Riots, Racism and Resistance in Imperial Britain*, (Liverpool: Liverpool University Press, 2009).

Loomba, Ania, *Colonialism/Post Colonialism*, (London: Routledge, 2010).

Marke, Ernest, *Old Man Trouble*, (London: Weidenfeld and Nicolson, 1975).

Murphy, Andrea, *From Empire to Rialto: Racism and Reaction in Liverpool 1918-1948*, (Liverpool: Liverpool University Press, 1995).

Nassy Brown, Jacqueline, *Dropping Anchor, Setting Sail: Geographies of Race in Black Liverpool* (Princeton: Princeton University Press, 1994).

Newsinger, John, *The Blood Never Dried: A People's History of the British Empire*, (London: Bookmarks, 2006).

Olusoga, David, *Black and British: A Forgotten History*, (Kindle Edition: Pan, 2016).

Paul, Kathleen, *Whitewashing Britain: Race and Citizenship in the Post War Era*, (NY: Cornell University Press, 1997).

Rediker, Marcus, *The Slave Ship: A Human History*, (London: John Murray, 2007).

Rennie, Simon, *The Poetry of Ernest Jones, Myth, Song, and the 'Mighty Mind'* (Cambridge: Routledge, 2016).

Rodney, Walter, *How Europe Underdeveloped Africa* (London: African Tree Press, 2014).

Rosenberg, Chanie, *1919: Britain on the Brink of Revolution* (London: Bookmarks, 1987).

Lord Scarman, *The Scarman Report: The Brixton Disorders 10-12 April 1981* (London: Pelican,1982).

Spry Rush, Anne, *Bonds of Empire: West Indians and Britishness from Victoria to Decolonization*, (Oxford: Oxford University Press, 2011).

Walvin, James, *England, Slaves and Freedom, 1776-1838*, (London: Macmillan, 1986).

Journal articles

Christian, Mark, 'The Fletcher Report 1930: A Historical Case Study of Contested Black Mixed Heritage Britishness', *Journal of Historical Sociology* Vol. 21 No. 2/3 June/September 2008 ISSN 0952-1909.

Jenkinson, Jaqueline, *The 1919 Race Riots in Britain: Their Background and Consequences*, For the Degree of Doctor of Philosophy (University of Edinburgh, 1987).

May, Roy & Robin Cohen, 'The Interaction Between Race and Colonialism: A Case Study of the Liverpool Race Riots of 1919', *Race and Class*, 16, 2 (1974).

Rowe, Michael, 'Sex, Race and Riot in Liverpool 1919', *Immigrants and Minorities Historical Studies in Ethnicity, Migration and Diaspora*, 19, 2 (2000).

Websites

Ahmed, Talat, 'The British Empire and the First World War: The Colonial Experience', *International Socialist Journal* 152 http://isj.org.uk/the-british-empire-and-the-first-world-war-the-colonial-experience/.

Belchem, John, 'Shock City: Sailortown Liverpool', *English Heritage,* https://content.historicengland.org.uk/images-books/publications/on-the-waterfront/waterfront-part2.pdf/.

BBC *Forbidden Riots* (1994) https://www.youtube.com/watch?v=6Pc-SVZhyG0.

Centenary News, *First World War, 1914-1918*
http://www.centenarynews.com/article?id=3262.

Elder Dempster Lines, *The History of Elder Dempster*
http://www.rakaia.co.uk/assets/elder-dempster-history-summary.pdf.

Frost, Diane & Richard Phillips, 'The 2011 Summer Riots: Learning from History - Remembering '81', *Sociological Research Online*, 17 (3) 19, <http://www.socresonline.org.uk/17/3/19.html>10.5153/sro.2718.

Guyana.net. *The Bookers Empire*, http://www.guyana.org/features/guyanastory/chapter112.html.

The National Archives, *Black Presence, Introduction: Arriving In Britain*
http://www.nationalarchives.gov.uk/pathways/blackhistory/intro/intro.htm.

University College London, *Legacies of British Slave Ownership*, London, https://www.ucl.ac.uk/lbs/.

Wikipedia, *The Death of Alan Kurdi*,
https://en.wikipedia.org/wiki/Death_of_Alan_Kurdi.

YouGov160118, 'British Empire', 18th January 2016
https://d25d2506sfb94s.cloudfront.net/cumulus_uploads/document/95euxfgway/InternalResults_160118_BritishEmpire_Website.pdf.

Newspapers

Alexander, Saffron, 'Windrush Generation: 'They thought we should be planting bananas',' *The Times*, 22nd June 2015.

Smith, Reiss, 'How could the Home Office age check Calais migrant 'children' from dental records?', *Daily Express*, 19th October 2016.

Primary Sources

Liverpool Records Office (LRO)

Great War to Race Riots Archive

13th May 1919, Letter from the Lord Mayor to the Secretary of the Colonial Office.

31st May 1919, Letter from Joseph Hall to the Lord Mayor.

3rd June 1919, Letter from Town Hall Clerk to Joseph Hall.

13th June 1919, Postcard from PS Lyon to The Lord Mayor.

2nd July 1919, Letter from The Presbyterian Church to the Lord Mayor of Liverpool.

2nd July 1919, Letter from Elisha Sterling to Lord Mayor of Liverpool.

7th October 1919, Letter from Edward R. Pickmere Esq, Town Clerk Liverpool to the Under Secretary of State.

20th October 1919, Extract from minutes from Legislate Council of Victoriaborg, Accra to Lord Mayor of Liverpool.

6th September 1920 Letter from Lord Mayor to H Maxwell of the Home Office.

11th September 1920 (b), List supplied by the African Christian Association for Lord Mayor of Liverpool.

28th September 1920, Unsigned letter to Lord Mayor of Liverpool.

7th October 1920, Letter JA Devitt Martyn, Secretary of the African Christian Association, to the Lord Mayor of Liverpool.

Watch Committee Minutes

17th June 1919, Letter from the Committee of the Africa Trade Section of the Liverpool Chamber of Commerce to Lord Mayor of Liverpool.

24th June 1919, Report of the Head Constable on the Race Riots to the Liverpool Watch Committee.

National Archives (NA)

Colonial Office (CO)

29th May 1919, CO 323 819, Internal Memorandum, Home Office.

12 June 1919, CO 323 814, Letter from Society of Peoples of African Origin to Secretary of State for the Colonies.

23rd June 1919, CO323/814-283 Memorandum on the Repatriation of Coloured Men.

25 July 1919, CO 318/349, Letter from Johnstone, Acting Governor of Jamaica, to the Colonial Office.

14th August 1919, CO 137/733, Confidential dispatch from Acting Governor Johnstone of Jamaica to Colonial Office.

3rd October 1919, CO 318 350, Colonial Office internal memorandum.

Home Office (HO)

10th June 2019, HO45 11017 2, Letter from Lionel Everett, Assistant Head Constable to the Under Secretary of State.

11th June 1919, HO 45 11017 7, Letter from the Office of the Superintending Alien Officer to HM Inspector.

12th June 1919, HO 45 170, Letter from Edward Shortt, Home Secretary to Herbert Creedy.

17th June 1919, HO 45 1017, Handwritten note from the Head Constable.

18th June 1919, HO45 11017, Letter from Home Office Civil Servant to Liverpool's Chief Constable.

26th June 1919, HO 45 11017, Report from Inspector Burgess, CIB to Home Office.

June 1919, NA, HO 45 11017, Telegram from Lionel Everett, Assistant Head Constable to the Under Secretary of State. (precise date not visible).